POEMS TO READ
WHEN YOU RUN OUT OF WEED

Paul Jeffrey Davids

POEMS TO READ WHEN YOU RUN OUT OF WEED

Second Edition Published by
Yellow Hat Publishing
A Division of Yellow Hat Productions, Inc.
5190 Neil Road #430
Reno, Nevada 89502

First Printing (First Edition) May 2012

First Printing (Second Edition) February 2013

ISBN 978-0-9890242-0-4

This book is dedicated to my children, Jordan Davids Duvall and Scott Michael Davids. They have both excelled in their professions and have made fine choices in life. And both, fortunately, are out of weed (and hopefully will stay that way), which leaves them with a little more time to read poetry.

Foreword

You don't need to be stoned on weed in order to get a big buzz from the poetry in this book. In fact, that's the whole point. You've found a far more effective form of entertainment. And if you are one of those who uses medicinal marijuana, try this medicinal poetry instead. Each poem has been hand-crafted as a profound and inspired labor of love designed to extinguish your existential crisis and give you a literary high – literally. Hopefully, these poems are destined for destiny and will outlast the Future War on Literature that Ray Bradbury predicted in FAHRENHEIT 451.

So enjoy yourself -- and just remember: No one has ever discovered a cure for addiction to poetry. But why would you want one? And if you take your time, soon you'll be thinking in rhyme all the time – and you'll feel fine and that will be quite sublime. You see, rhythmic rhymes have started to take over your mind already, and you've only just arrived at the Table of Contents!

Table of Contents

1. THE BIG BANG

Creation, they say, was created
When nothingness suddenly abated
The questions of why and how
Are not answered right now
But physicists when they lecture
Are likely to conjecture
That everything we know
Throughout the vastness of space
Was once so tiny
You could not find a trace

Of course you were not here then
And neither was I
This was thirteen billion years
Before Earth, wind and sky

Smaller than an atom it was
Until it exploded
Because it was loaded
With stuff that became bloated

Well, actually, we don't really know
What caused it to grow
But in the blink of God's eye
The Big Bang grew nigh

It was an explosion long past
But an explosion so very vast
That reason does desist
And the mind will resist
Conceiving the moment
When Creation did foment
What we call the Big Bang
When God first sang

Paul Jeffrey Davids

This cosmic soup we can't fathom
At a time when not a single atom
Existed at all
You know, my mind hits a wall
As I try to conceive
God's cosmic weave

In physics theories that they trot
They say it was too hot
For atoms to be
Let alone you or me
But in millions of years
At a time of no fears
The quark was the article
A sub-atomic particle
Supreme above all
But there was nothing at all
Except quarks and perhaps light
But it was an eternal night
Did I express this quite right?
Well, God had foresight!

And somehow or other
As God's wits did recover
He cooled it all down
And atoms came around

And as the years became billions
Across a vastness of zillions
Of miles of nothing
Well, then there was something

Hydrogen, which is
I assure you sir and madam
The very tiniest
atom

THE BIG BANG

Helium
Atom number two
Which makes balloons float
At the zoo

And more atoms that will last forever
That sprang up from – well, whatever
Made up of the proton and electron
This is Truth, not a con

Then stars began to form
When God blew his horn
And then galaxies swirled
As God whirled and twirled

Some stars exploded
And these stars were loaded
In the galactic kettle
With heavy metal

Like silver and gold
Those elements are old
And arsenic and lead
They can both make you dead

In the beginning atoms did mingle
In the great cosmic tingle
And molecules were born
In the great cosmic storm

The stars then did spew
The stuff that became you
Better include me too
But the story's not through

Because between then and now
Billions of years somehow
Transpired and conspired
To create the cat and the cow

But first came the galaxies
With arms over-reaching
Each with billions of stars
As God was beseeching
Those stars to spew planets
From their fiery core
Are you following this, I hope?
It is all scientific gospel lore

Then from those planets
Solar systems gave birth
To astronomical motions
That included our Earth

The Earth, like a grain of sand
On an endless cosmic beach
Is barely a speck
This is what scientists teach

To have perspective is to know
That all this is so
But how did life grow?
And why does it come and go?

For the answers you can choose
Between science and religions
Or just admit you'll never know
And then go feed the pigeons

2. Y2K - THE DAY OF RECKONING

Y2K was the time
That the millennium would arrive
The year two thousand
When civilization would thrive

But it was our terrible fate
That no arrangements for that date
Had been made in any which way
So lots of bucks we had to pay

We were told time and again
It would be a terrible moment when
That new year arrived
And everything for which we'd strived
Would all fall apart
And from scratch we'd have to start
Unless we would dare
To undertake a big repair

Yes, it was soon to be Y2K
A day that couldn't go away
Without disaster coming to stay
And everyone's nerves would fray

For they told us in voices stern
That a sad lesson we would learn
Because technology was frail
And all computers would fail

We'd be clean out of luck
With computers all getting stuck
Because none could display
Yes, even if everyone would pray
The number two for that new year
That much was clear

Two thousand was soon in store
It was not nineteen hundred anymore
Our tempers would get hot
Like it or not

And the costs they would hike
A fact no one would like
For to fix the dilemma
Would be worse than an enema

And before the dawn of that day
How we'd all have to pay
And then pay once again
Every night and every day

And so billions were expended
And our confidence upended
Because if computers shut down
In every city and town
There'd be no way, you know
To make anything go

The techies got rich
Because of this mess
But their brains were insufficient
They all did confess

And the churches didn't help
Nor would God bless
Because on the Seventh Day
He began His long rest

Y2K - THE DAY OF RECKONING

Was the problem really so complex?
Were they playing with full decks?
They demanded to be paid
More often than a prostitute gets laid

They drained our assets dry
Until we all wanted to cry
Bankrupt and broke
We started to choke
But thank them we would
Because maybe they could
End the confusion
Caused by the mass delusion

Y2K came and went
With hardly a flutter
And all our computers
Worked smoother than butter

There was never an issue
Worth such despair
There was no major problem
That demanded repair

But the amount that we spent
To make the "problem" disappear
Was rather like taking
A stiff pole up the rear

3. STRIPE, THE KITTEN

Kyle did not know
From where the cat came
It had no collar
No evidence of a name

The mew that cat mewed
Was rather subdued
The pleading look in his eye
Made Kyle want to cry

Yes, here was a kitty
So fair and pretty
That when it clawed with a paw
At Kyle's stately front door
Kyle looked down and saw
The kitty that filled him with awe

But it was not to be
That Kyle's home would be free
To either dog or kitty
Who dropped by to see
Whether the door would stay open
That's what the kitty was hopin'
But Kyle needed no pet
A pet would make him fret

He told the kitty "No, no,
Please, you must go"
And so the kitty then left
Leaving Kyle bereft

STRIPE, THE KITTEN

For Kyle lived alone
With his TV and phone
His newspaper and books
And chess -- bishops and rooks
That he moved across the board
Trying not to be bored
At his friendless life
Yes, Kyle had no wife

It was the very next day
Bright and early, I'd say
When Kyle opened the door
The kitty scampered across the floor
That cat had returned
Its love was not to be spurned

It jumped in one leap
Onto a chair as if to keep
For itself that fine spot
Comfortable? Yes, quite a lot

"No, no," said Kyle
Trying not to smile
"Don't make yourself at home
I live here all alone
I don't want a new pet
And my gosh, you're all wet!"

Out the window he glanced
While the cat leaped and pranced
It was raining very hard
So Kyle played a new card

"You can stay a few hours
While I trim some flowers
To make a bouquet
To brighten my day

But when the rain shall end
Then I shall not spend
Another minute with you
I've important things to do
You'll go back to where you came
And if it again starts to rain
Do not return
That's a lesson to learn"

The kitty did mew
As if it knew
Exactly what Kyle
Intended to do

But the Kitty had
Ideas of his own
And his idea
Was to live in this home

As Kyle snipped flowers
He mustered his powers
Of conversation, polite
Keeping the kitty in sight

It was Kyle's choice
To speak in a soft voice:
"My name is Kyle
And I rarely smile
Especially at cats
I don't like their naps
They relax and they yawn
So do not spawn
My anger or alarm
With your sweet kitten charm
When the clock strikes one
Your time here is done
Whether rain or shine
You'll depart and that's fine"

STRIPE, THE KITTEN

The cat did brush
Up against Kyle's leg
It mewed and it stared
One could say, it begged

"No, no, I won't feed you,"
Said Kyle in a huff
"If I feed you you'll want to stay
Oh, it's nice how you fluff
You're quite soft, I see
And you seem to like me
But I will not pet you
That's what I must not do
For if affection I show
Then you'll never go
And my solitary life here
Will be over, I fear"

Well, the cat looked quite fetchin'
As it sprang to the kitchen
And looked all around
Hardly making a sound

And then again spoke Kyle
Suppressing a smile:
"If you could talk
I'd ask you your name
But cats don't speak
So let's play a game
I'll guess your name
And if I get it right
Go hide in the pantry
And get out of sight"

They played the game
For almost an hour
The rain didn't stop
It continued to shower

"Are you Lambert or Perry
Or Chatworth or Jerry?
Are you Beeswax or Fred
Or Tiger or Ted?
Perhaps you are Jergin
Or Firefox or Perkin?
Or Flimfam or Fipe
Or Corman or Stripe?"

At the word Stripe
The kitten did creep
To hide in the pantry
And then it did leap
Because Stripe wanted to eat
He jumped up with his feet
To a shelf that had snacks
Leaving muddy tracks
In that pantry so neat
Kyle said: "Let me repeat
There's no food for you
Eating's not what you'll do"

But Stripe's behavior was unreal
He was already consuming a meal
On the shelf covered with vinyl
Stripe's decision was final
He had decided to live here
And he'd have no fear
Of objections from Kyle
Who didn't care for Stripe's style

But Stripe had selected this home
He had chosen this estate
And Kyle would have no say
Because this was his fate
And a man is never the master
Of his house
The kitten is the master
And the man can just grouse

STRIPE, THE KITTEN

Kyle indeed felt great confusion
But Stripe arrived at this conclusion:
Kyle was a bother
Rather like a weak father
But Stripe would train him
To behave just right
Stripe would tolerate him
And keep him in sight
And signal him when
It was time for Stripe to eat
And when to buy cat food
And how to be sweet
And when to fetch
Stripe's favorite pillow
And then Stripe would nap
Beneath the large willow
Sometimes barely stirring
Not tossing to and fro
Dreaming of the life
He wanted to know
But then Kyle was shouting
"Go, Kitty, go!"

Like a knight anointed
To the door Kyle pointed
His castle he would defend
And Stripe's comfort upend

"Go, Kitty, go!
And don't you be slow!
From my pantry you steal
This is quite unreal
You act as though it's you
Who rules this house"
And that was the instant
That Stripe first heard the mouse

The mouse, it scampered
Right across the floor
Right in front of Kyle
Heading for the door
But Stripe did leap
It was quite a feat
With his strength, every ounce
On that mouse he did pounce

The mouse was so fearful
He squeaked and was tearful
Stripe kept him between his paws
Trapped by his claws

"My goodness, I thank you"
Said Kyle, satisfied
"If I'd seen a mouse in the house
We'll, I'd nearly have died
So I see that perhaps
You might earn your keep
You'll hunt the mice
Every night while I sleep"

So startled beyond measure
Kyle had voiced his pleasure
It was the end of round one
And Stripe – well, he'd won!

"A pet's not such a bad thing"
Said Kyle, his voice firm
"Stripe, you'll be of good use
If some lessons you learn
Never shall you wake me
Because I like my sleep
Never shall you shake me
From dreams that are deep
When I want you outside
Then outside you'll go
And if company visits

STRIPE, THE KITTEN

Then your face you won't show
And when I command silence
Then you'll never mew
And when the newspaper I read
You won't chew on my shoe
And if I don't want to play
Then you'll go away
Do we have the rules straight?
Good, then you can stay!"

It wouldn't be easy
That much Stripe knew
He'd have to train Kyle
By chewing on his shoe

Stripe would chase birds
While Kyle did sleep
And Stripe would wake him
When Stripe was ready to eat

How would Stripe tell Kyle
That tuna and salmon were best?
How would he tell Kyle
Not to be a pest?
How would he show Kyle
That rugs were for clawing?
When would Kyle buy cat toys
Especially for pawing?

And catnip, oh yes!
That was surely needed
And digging up lawns
That were newly seeded

And so it came to pass
As day followed night
That Kyle soon learned
To give up the fight

Try as he might
To claim his favorite chair
Kyle didn't dare
If Stripe was already there

For the chair that was soft
With nice arms so round
Was the chair where Stripe
Without making a sound
Would curl up and dream
For an hour and a day
And Kyle was trained
Not to get in the way

In fact Kyle got the point
That Stripe loved fish
Especially when served
In a big cat dish

And Kyle never dared
To trim Kitty's claws
Those were the rules
Those were Stripe's laws

And the chess pieces that stood
On the chessboard in the hall
Were there for one reason
So Stripe could make them fall

He'd leap to attack
Those bishops and knights
And Kyle never dared
To put up a fight

Kyle learned his place
In Stripe's stately home
One human could not live there
All alone

STRIPE, THE KITTEN

Cats? Oh, there'd be many
Who'd come over to play
They'd drop in any time
And any old day

And Kyle would clean up
When the party was over
And the dog next door?
The dog named Rover?
Stripe screeched in his ears
And leaped on his back
Stripe scratched him and lashed him
As he made his attack

Rover ran away
That was such a fine day
And that's when more cats
Soon stopped by to play

At first there were three
Kyle thought, how can this be?
And when he saw ten
Kyle had such a yen
To throw all the cats out
With a very loud shout

Kyle's life was sad now
Life was no fun
But Stripe made it clear
When Kyle was to come
And when Kyle was to sit
And when Kyle was to serve
As Stripe's man-servant
Kyle should never swerve
From his duties so clear
And his chores, one and all
Because Stripe the kitten
Now ruled over all!

4. THE MAN WITHOUT HAIR

Never was there
A man without hair
Until Reginald McBeaver
Came down with a fever
And with his eyes a red glare
While seated in a chair
He stopped to stare
In a mirror too long
While humming a sad song
He didn't know it was wrong
Well, maybe he did
But his hair he did bid
To stay in its place
While he made a grim face
And then out of his briefcase
He took a bottle of stuff
So his hair he could muss

He took the risk
After a girl he had kissed
Told him he'd be stuffy
If his hair wasn't fluffy

Bald men did not exist
When Reggie made his list
Of all the Old Wives Tales
That should never be missed
And there was one legend strange:
Staring in a mirror can rearrange
The scalp of a man
Who lacks a suntan
And then his hair all drops out
Causing him to shout

THE MAN WITHOUT HAIR

If in a mirror you stare
And then lose your hair
Then whoever you meet
While walking in the street
If he stares back at you
Well, then his hairy days are through
For his hair will also fall out
Of that there can be little doubt

So Reggie started an epidemic
Of a malady systemic
Baldness spread far and wide
Old wives tales never lied
For if he merely glanced at you
You wouldn't know what to do
As your hair began to fall like rain
Causing you substantial pain

A wig you could wear
But who would it fool?
A hat you'd put on
As a general rule
But you'd be an outcast
Because your hair wouldn't last
And Reggie was to blame
Oh, the shame! The shame!

No bald men at all
Had existed before
But now the plague spread
And Reggie did dread
Walking anywhere
Where he might stare
At a man unsuspecting
Who would experience unrelenting
Loss of his hair
Or perhaps a lady quite fair
Would then lose her hair

The baldness plight
Got Reggie into a fight
And the baldness that did ensue
Left him in a stew
As a hundred men did sue
And a hundred women too
And I assure you this is true

Who am I?—you may ask
Such that I make this claim
Well, it's not important
That you know my name
But I am an officer
Of the law
Used to be the most dashing man
You ever saw
But something befell me
Now you dare not see
What's become of my hair
Which exists nowhere
Neither here nor there
Not anywhere
I lost my hair
Because of Reginald's stare
There are days that I dread
And won't get out of bed

Well, Reginald was arrested
Though all blame he contested
But my prisoner is to blame
That I feel shame
My hair was my glory
So I've told you this story

I took the mirror
Out of Reggie's cell
I told him not to look at me
He didn't look well

THE MAN WITHOUT HAIR

And within two weeks
We all had the creeps
For all the officers of the law
Suddenly dropped their jaws
Because their hair fell out
It was a rout

And even in City Hall
The hair did fall
And finally Reggie accepted blame
Before one and all

"I'm sorry," said Reggie
"Forgive me, oh please
I didn't mean to cause this
I am down on my knees
If I could do something
To repent
My sorrow indeed
Would be sorrow well spent
For hair is wonderful
To have on one's head
 So you took me prisoner
And my rights you then read
But I meant no one any harm
Or to spread such alarm
Please send me to a farm
Where I'll use all my charm
To grow lots of corn
And then I won't be forlorn
For if you eat corn
Hair follicles are born
And they grow and grow
Until no one will know
Who you might be
Because your face they can't see
You'll have so much hair
That a hat you can't wear

He made a good case
With a sweet look on his face
And so we freed him from jail
With his face oh-so-pale
And to a farm he did go
So his corn he could grow

And when on corn we did feast
Our hair grew like yeast
It's wonderful but....
IT'S HAIR YOU CAN'T CUT!

5. TECHNOLOGY BITES

Try though he might
To be firm and upright
And all his energy to conserve
Cyrus didn't deserve
This situation that was grave
For to everything he gave
Himself, head to toe
And that brought him low
And sorrowed him so

His energy got sucked
Even if he ducked
And went back to bed
To sort of play dead

For no matter where he turned
His need for peace was spurned
And trouble was churned
Cyrus never learned

It began with the clock
When he awoke
Something inside him
Shook as he spoke

"I want to sleep more!"
He screamed at the clock
The clock beeped quite loud
And he was in shock

It rattled his brain
And left him in pain
And because of that clock
His energy did wane

Then came the TV
To get the weather
Before it came on
He felt light as a feather
But then he felt heavy
Burdened by news
There were robberies, murders
It gave him the blues

There were typhoons and wars
Drug addicts by the scores
Con-men and whores
Rotten to their cores

It was no way to wake up
Being a slave to that TV
Especially since it showed
Stuff he didn't want to see

He hated all those ads
That tried to sell Cyrus stuff
And he didn't care for reality shows
When his reality was quite enough

And the noise, the sonic boom
From that TV that filled the room
Yes, all those shows with phony shtick
He tired of those shows so quick

The best thing about the TV
Was the remote control in his hand
So he could turn it off at once
When he saw things he couldn't stand

After TV came the stove
To warm up the tea kettle
He turned on the burner
And the stove tested his mettle

TECHNOLOGY BITES

Because the annoying thing
Was when the kettle would sing
That meant it was boiling
And for Cyrus that meant spoiling
His peaceful meditation
Of cosmic vibration
Yes, his concentration was done
When the kettle had sung

The next challenge was turning
Bread into toast
If the toaster didn't pop up
The whole kitchen would roast

And that toaster!
Well, it might blow a fuse
And then Cyrus
Would swiftly accuse
The toaster store
Of causing much more
Damage than he ever dreamed
At least so it seemed

And to really enjoy his toast
There was much more in store
Because he had to open
His refrigerator door
For the butter to fetch
Oh, he felt like a wretch
Because to open the door
Required much more
Determination and force
Than he had, of course

And the butter was never cold
Because the refrigerator was old
Nothing but trouble would enfold
If only that refrigerator he had sold!

Paul Jeffrey Davids

Then he booted up his computer
That was his next maneuver
For booting up, you wait
And that always makes you late

There's no great sensation
When the Internet's on vacation
Or if Microsoft Word
Flips you the bird

And you might find your missing file
That was there all the while
But all your folders have vanished
And you're still feeling famished
Because toast is not sufficient
For food you'll be persistent
But you don't want eggs and bacon
And you don't feel like makin'
Anything around you can see
And the tea tastes like pee
And that last awful TV ad
Made you feel so bad
That you don't want to eat
You're suffering from defeat
And you're about to raise a stink
Because you're out of printer ink
And the paper's all used up
So you're feeling rather stuck

And then you want to make a call
But you're not feeling on the ball
Because there's no connection for Verizon
It's vanished beyond the horizon
And you've lost your I-Phone
It's left you all alone
And your land line is quite dead
You need a bullet for your head
To blow your brains out neatly
And depart the Earth quite sweetly

6. FOOD FOR THOUGHT

If it ever happens
That you should have a thought
You'll probably need to feed it
With food that can't be bought

Thoughts always feed
On ideas in need
Of nourishment and energy
And imagination's the seed

Then your thought will grow
You'll become all aglow
And fresh ideas will sprout
All about

But the problem with ideas
Is they lead to things quite drastic
Sometimes ideas
Can even make you enthusiastic

Enthusiasm requires energy
And energy requires food
And if you don't chew on an idea
You'll end up in a horrible mood

Chewed-on ideas
Sometimes you can swallow
But if your idea escapes you
You may feel quite hollow

So if it ever happens
That you should have a thought
Be careful what you wish for
You may get what you sought

7. ANITA, THE ANGELFISH

Anita the Angelfish was on trial
Her beliefs were not worthwhile
They were false, in fact
Her claims were a big act

She fluttered before her judge
Above a dark floor of slimy sea sludge
The coral court was all festooned
Anita was sure to be doomed

She believed fish were not alone
An idea that would sink like a stone
She claimed that beyond the glass wall
Creatures quite tall
Were providing fish with food
To keep fish in a good mood
And the providers -- those creatures
With very strange features
Lived in a world beyond the wall
So the fish world was not all

Lucas the glowfish was the magistrate
Who would determine Anita's fate
For every fish did know
Even fish who didn't glow
That the universe did end
At those glass walls that couldn't bend
And there was nothing beyond
Of this idea all fish were fond

For the Great Creator Fish unseen
In ancient times had a great dream
And from that dream he did make
The undersea lake

ANITA, THE ANGELFISH

There was a glass wall on each side
Beyond which nothing could hide
Or even exist
For Creator Fish had a list
With the name of every fish
That ever was or would be
Living in the aquarium – the Fish Sea

To speak of a world outside the wall
Was forbidden – a fish must not call
Nor shout out in the vain wish
That there was a world of non-fish
To speak of non-fish was nonsense
That made the magistrate very tense

It simply was not appealing
To speak of a world above the ceiling
High above there was nothing
And the very idea of something
Beyond Aquarium water that exists
Well, a fish would have to desist
Before uttering such a thought
Unless death was what that fish sought

Anita the Angelfish – well, nervous was she
As she claimed that with her eyes she did see
A creature, something called a child
With eyes and a whole face that smiled
And the child was not alone
There were other walls perhaps made of stone
And doors and lights and creatures called men
Perhaps as many as ten
Or maybe many more
In that outer room with a floor
And a ceiling so high
Far beyond where fish live and die

"Oh enough!" stammered the magistrate
He said: "I will now firmly state
The rules of our religion we all know
So don't outrage us so
There's nothing but fish and one snail
There is no Other Side of the Veil
There is Creator Fish
Who had a great wish
That we should live
And so life He did give
But this glass box was created for us
Anita, you make me so mad I could cuss
Because you tell such a weird tale
I shall sentence you now to jail
To the coral cage you shall go
And that is far down below
And you'll stay there forever
Or until whenever
You recant and repent
That's how your days will be spent"

But that was when
Giant fingers – all ten
Could be seen at a wall
And a creature tall
(A human girl, actually
That's what she was – factually)
Spoke in a strange voice cool
As if from a distant whirlpool

"Mother," said the smiling girl
"This aquarium is so much fun
It's a little world all its own
Watching fish, I'm never done
They are such little swishy things
I like them better than my swings
Just think, oceans have fish by the millions
Or better yet, maybe billions"

ANITA, THE ANGELFISH

Well, hearing that
Lucas the Magistrate almost died
And the other fish
Well, they simply cried

Lucas exclaimed: "None of that did we hear!
It did not reach any fish ear
And we take no glee
In what some think they might see
For we know for a fact
There is nothing like that
Nothing at all
Beyond the great wall
Our world alone does exist
All thoughts of oceans are dismissed!"

And so Anita, in spite of her plea
Was convicted of fish blasphemy
And to the coral jail she went
And many a day there spent
Wishing that some day
She might be set free
And wondering why other fish
The Truth could not see

8. ROY'S TOY

Roy was a boy
Whose room was a mess
He never cleaned up
He disobeyed, I confess

He hated when his parents
Popped in for inspections
Roy was a boy
Who never followed directions

That were problems at school
And also at home
And he talked for hours
On the phone

And he sometimes complained
About all the toys that he lacked
Things his parents refused to buy
And that was a fact

Now there was in Roy's house
A room with no reason
It had no purpose at all
In any season

When you stepped inside
Nothing made you laugh
It was not a bedroom
And it had no bath

The walls were all plain
And the ceiling too
And inside that room
There was nothing to do

ROY'S TOY

You could sit on the floor
You could lock the door
Windows? There were none
That room was no fun

Seldom did anyone
Go inside
And it remained that way
Until Roy went for a ride

One winter day
He rode his sleigh
And without taking a spill
Reached the bottom of the hill
And then the sky turned gray
What made it that way?

It snowed fiercely that day
And Roy lost his way
The whole world was white
There was nothing in sight

And this is no lie
He saw an elf in the sky
That elf spoke by and by
And what it had to say
On that cold winter day
Was no doubt perplexing
At times he was vexing
He spoke of Roy's Mom and Dad
And how Roy had been bad
When he didn't obey
But hey, that was Roy's way

The elf spoke of foxes and boxes
And things happening too soon
He spoke of doorknobs and locks
He talked of flowers in bloom

He spoke of marching bands
And castles and moats
Of a world upside down
And cranky old goats

The elf was mischievous
And looked quite strange
And Roy heard its voice
Say the word "REARRANGE"

The elf that he saw
Was brightly glowing
Roy asked the elf his name
Said the elf: "Far better not knowing
For if you know my name
Life will stay just the same
That would be a shame
So let's start the game"

Before the elf floated away
On that cold winter day
Roy heard the elf say
"YOU HAVE A NEW TOY – LET'S PLAY!"

But there was nothing at all
Except Roy and his sleigh
And snow so high
It reached up to the sky

So Roy left that hill
And went on his way
Wondering about the new toy
And wanting to play!

When he got home
Something wasn't the same
The room with no reason
Had a sign with his name

ROY'S TOY

It said "ROY'S PLAYROOM"
And outside was a broom
And the elf's voice sang a tune
He sang "DO NOT OPEN UNTIL JUNE"

But the door creaked open
Just one small crack
Roy peeked inside
He didn't look back

There were cobwebs inside
And also a box
The box was bigger than Roy
With a picture of a fox

His parents weren't home
He was all alone
He swept up with that broom
He cleaned the whole room

Beneath the fox were some words
That Roy noticed quite soon
Roy read the words
DO NOT OPEN UNTIL JUNE

It certainly wasn't June
And wouldn't be soon
How could he wait
For such a far away date?

Well, it was a big box to open
For such a young boy
But open it he did
And inside was THE TOY

It was a toy like nothing else
That he'd ever seen
Except for the toys
That appeared in his dreams

The toy was marvelous
The toy was grand
The toy was remarkable
The toy came with a band

A small band it was
With little toy men
They played and they marched
And then marched again

The band played tunes
That nobody knew
The toy started out small
And then it grew

His parents returned
They had questions to ask
And answering those questions
Proved to be a tough task

The room with no reason
Now had a lock on the door
Only Roy could open it
Said his parents: "What is this for?"

And they certainly noticed
The sign DO NOT OPEN UNTIL JUNE
And they quickly figured out
Roy opened the box much too soon

For the month of February
Was four months from June
Sixteen weeks in all
To stay out of that room

They did not know
That elves must be obeyed
Out of that room
Is where Roy should have stayed

ROY'S TOY

But it was too late to obey
The warning so strange
Which said: IF OPENED TOO SOON
EVERYTHING WILL REARRANGE

Roy's parents inspected
The box with the fox
And the sign and the toy
That had appeared for their boy

Yes, the toy had appeared
On that cold winter day
With a gift card for Roy
Inviting him to play

But if only he hadn't touched it
Like the sign said
Then nothing would have happened
To Roy's bed

The bed rose to the ceiling
And then it dropped
Two inches from the floor
It suddenly stopped

It hovered right there
A bit like a balloon
And all because Roy
Had acted too soon

"I don't like this a bit"
His mother did say
"We don't know who sent this
We should send it away"

"No, no, it's for me"
Roy firmly declared
"It has my name on the card
So don't be scared"

Paul Jeffrey Davids

"I don't think I trust it!"
His mother shouted
Roy made a sad face
He frowned and he pouted

"You don't follow directions"
Said his Mom and his Dad
"To ignore the instructions
Well – that's bad!"

But Roy played with the toy
And everything changed
As the warning said
The house REARRANGED

A couch simply vanished
His Mom was hardly ecstatic
Living room furniture
Then appeared in the attic

The stove in the kitchen
Became a dishwashing machine
The logs in the fireplace
Gave off steam

The ceiling became cloudy
It even sprinkled
The drapes on the windows
Suddenly all wrinkled

The car in the garage
Was now upside down
The clothes drying machine
Wouldn't go round

Flowers began to sprout
All over the yard
The pillows on the beds
Now had turned hard

ROY'S TOY

Roy's bed still hovered
And it leaped up to the loft
Then the bricks of the fireplace
All became soft

There was on Roy's toy
A lever to pull
Pulling on the lever
Turned Roy's clothes to wool

And the walls in the playroom
Turned from white to bright green
And then Roy disappeared
He couldn't be seen

Roy's father and mother
Were anything but charmed
I would describe them as being
Extremely alarmed

His father exclaimed
In a voice full of fear
"This toy is quite dangerous
Doomsday could be near!
Your index of refraction
Has become nil
There must be some cure
Perhaps some new pill!
You're the invisible boy
Because of this toy!"

Roy's mother decided
To speak with sweet grace
"This new toy in this room
Well, it is a disgrace!
If you're invisible now
Your hair we can't comb
Without our supervision
Where might you roam?

Paul Jeffrey Davids

We'll need a new rule
You can't go to school
What will they do
If they cannot see you?"

But no sooner did they
Both express their dismay
Roy became visible again
And continued to play

The band played on
Those tiny marching men
At first there were five
But soon there were ten

And to their surprise
In that room with no reason
It began to snow
Well, it was the season

They all got so cold
They needed their coats
But then off in the corner
There appeared several goats

And then much to their horror
And much to their shock
Roy began to float
They had to take stock

As Roy floated above
His father and mother
He laughed and he giggled
As they ducked for cover

What a startling situation
That they could not end
And then money snowed from the ceiling
And Roy wanted to spend

Said Roy: "With so much money
Life won't be a hassle
I know what I'll do
I'll buy us a castle
A castle so large
It will have two moats
And that's where they'll swim
These lovely new goats"

His father was angry
At this new toy
He spoke his mind plainly
He was not at all coy

"I do not want a toy
To completely rearrange
Our lives here so peaceful
Our lives were not strange
But now any moment
Impossible things
Happen at random
That goat – it sings!
And the band of little men
Of which there were ten
Now there are twenty!
Oh, when will this ever end?
I don't want to be rich
With funny money
We had love in this family
Yes, of love we had plenty
But now I no longer know
My ups from my downs
This odd new toy
Has turned us into clowns!"

No sooner did his father say that
With an enormous frown
His clothes at once changed
Into the clothes of a clown

His father's face it was painted
And his nose was a red ball
Roy then stopped floating
He began to fall

His mother caught him
And said full of dread
"Turn off this new toy
It's all gone to your head
This room with this snow
And this band and these goats
And this money from above
And our son who floats"

It was at that moment
They heard a chime
And on the back of the toy
They noticed a sign

The letters were so small
They had to squint
It said: TO RETURN TO NORMAL
PUSH THE HANDLE AND SPRINT

The handle they saw
But to push it or not?
Would the money then vanish?
There was such a lot!

Said Roy: "This toy we won't share
With our neighbors and friends
Who don't like strange stuff
And don't go for new trends
This has been splendid
Yes, it has been fun
But I will push on the handle
And with a sprint I'll run"

ROY'S TOY

The handle he pushed down
And then his father wasn't a clown
And the goats were no more
What else was in store?
No money could be seen
Was this all a dream?

Roy sprinted around
Going real fast
And the strange rearrangements
Well, they didn't last

You wonder about the marching band?
Those tiny men could no longer stand
The musicians all fell to the floor
And then they fled out the door

They vanished in an instant
And so did the toy
And Roy's Mom and Dad
Were overcome with great joy

Said Roy's Dad: "I don't know
What elf you did meet
And if I ever saw him
Well, that elf I would greet
But I'd tell him quite plainly
So he'd understand
That we have no use
For a marching band
All we want
Is to be happy together
In snow or rain
Or any old weather
And as for the rest
We don't need such a toy
All we need
Is to have our fine boy"

9. THE CAT AND THE MOUSE

There was a girl who had a house
And in the house there was a mouse
And outside the house there was a cat
Life is sometimes just like that

And this is what transpired
The cat and the mouse conspired
That the cat would chase the mouse
All around that house
But he would not catch the mouse

But one day while the cat slept
That mouse crept
And jumped on the cat
Right on its back
And the cat leaped in fright
And could not sleep that night
For his terrible fears
That always brought tears
Were fears of mice
Mice not nice
Mice that turned to ice
And would freeze a cat
Yes, cat dreams are like that

So amidst the flora and fauna
Outside the house by the sauna
The poor cat lived in trauma
The cat's fears grew and grew
That the little mouse he knew
Would jump on him anew
And scratch his back and pull his hair
Yes, very easily this cat did scare

THE CAT AND THE MOUSE

The cat stayed by himself
While the mouse practiced stealth
And though the mouse was fat
He still hunted that cat
And though the mouse was slow
The cat's fears did grow
Hiding under a canopy
That cat needed therapy

The girl loved the cat
And she wasn't happy that
The cat was so sad
Because that mouse had been bad
And the cat feared for its life
And spent its days in fright

The girl had a Dad she called Pappy
Who was loving and made it snappy
At answering to her every need
With the greatest of speed

It was a fact that her Dad
Was not at all glad
To see the cat so upset
And when it rained the cat got wet
And wouldn't come inside
Because that mouse might ride
Around on his back
Cats can be like that

Pappy was a therapist
Who was a cat specialist
And he had a cat couch
And toward the cat he would crouch
And they'd talk over the issue
The cat cried, needed tissue

"Be reasonable," Pappy said
"The mouse doesn't want you dead
The mouse is your friend
And his days he wants to spend
Playing with you
That's what he wants to do
Therefore, to jump on your back
Is not an attack
It's an expression of love
That is blessed from above
It's his way to embrace
And show you his grace
He will not bite you
Nor will he fight you
I talked to the mouse
And he begs you not to grouse
The mouse made that confession
So snap out of your depression"

Well, it worked, one, two, three
At last the cat did see
That it was far too callous
To assume the mouse acted with malice
And the girl was so happy
At the success of Pappy
That her Pappy she hugged
And his heartstrings she tugged

10. OLD STUFF

Furniture is like people
It ages and becomes feeble
And you should not ration
Your love and compassion
For furniture that's broken
That yearns for a token
Of feeling and concern
And from that you should learn
That all furniture beneath ceilings
Has sensitive feelings

"They think we're just old stuff,"
Said the sad lamp to the armchair
"At least you have a dust-cover
Something you can wear
But my lampshade is torn
And my cord is worn
They keep me unplugged
On this tattered rug
And I'm covered with dust
And beginning to rust"

"I too feel my age"
Said the armchair like a sage
"My left arm is loose
From when I served in a caboose
I enjoyed life on that train
Except when it would rain
It would get so damp
I'd get an awful cramp
When someone plopped down
Into my seat that's round
On my pillow that needs stitching
And lately I've been itching"

Then the empty bookshelf did creak
And said in a timid voice quite meek
"I live in constant fear
That they'll throw us away
And don't get too confident
It could happen any day
Oh, I used to have a hundred books
And that gave me very fine looks
I was a handsome devil
And all my shelves were level
But now the darn Kindle
Has made the number of my books dwindle
Yes, I think it's almost become my time
I heard our owner say that I'm next in line"

"Next in line – for what?"
From the dresser the question came
But the dresser already knew the answer
It was always the same

"Next in line for a trip to the dump"
The bookshelf said like a somber grump
"As with people, so it is with us
We fall apart, and then it's over because
To a hospital they don't send us
And there's no rescue in a truck
They won't repair us
And we're out of luck"

"Age befits me well,"
Replied the desk, a fine roll-top
They've used me for fifty years
And they'll never stop
My wood has fine grain
And I'm quite the same
As in the days I was new
Of decades – I've seen a few!
And I'll see several more
Then I'll be four-score

OLD STUFF

Which means eighty
A term quite weighty
That Lincoln in his own way
At Gettysburg did say
 Yes, you're all broken and rusty
And non-functional, dusty
A better life you seek
But you're not oak or teak
And of self-pity you reek
But me? I'm unique
Come on, take a peek
Look at me – an antique!"

"In value antiques grow"
Said the lamp who did know
That never again would he glow
And off to the dump he would go

And the bookshelf's life?
Its days were spent in strife
Because soon they would slice
Him into pieces – not nice
And they'd use him for lumber
It was nigh, his eternal slumber

And the armchair lived in alarm
Sure to lose the broken arm
Perhaps his existence would stop
How he envied the roll-top

Well, this poem has some morals
So let's not rest upon our laurels
And if furniture is what you are
When you wish upon a star
If it's eternal life for which you resolve
You'd better hope that you will evolve
Into a distinguished and rather sleek
Antique!

11. ATTENTION DEFICIT DISORDER

I have Attention Deficit Disorder
Which means my attention span is shorter
Pass that juice, please
No, not the teas
I want coffee with my sugar
Blow your nose if you have a booger

You see, that's the way it is
My mind is like soda fizz
My concentration is hardly in order
My focus flits right at the border
Of here and there
Or anywhere
So please excuse me if
The subject changes in a jiff

What movies are playing in 3-D?
Where's the Mens' Room, I have to pee!
Am I getting old? Is that a gray hair?
You there, lady! Do not stare!

And you there, reader!
Your eyes are not on this page!
Are you paying attention to me?
If not, you'll taste my rage
So you're starting to see much quicker
That my concentration does flitter
Here and there
And everywhere
Check out the sky
Is that a speck in my eye?

ATTENTION DEFICIT DISORDER

There was a time when I did flower
I had extraordinary will power
I could concentrate for an hour
But then life – well, it began to sour

Did I tell you that I concentrate shorter?
Because I have Attention Deficit Disorder
Maybe I said that
I can't remember
I think I came down with it
Last December
When six of my friends went with me
To the videogame jamboree

Moving my thumbs with the speed of a jet
My eyes on the games for two days, and yet
Something happened deep in my brain
Maybe a mental muscle that I did sprain
I lost the ability to concentrate
Maybe because I over-ate
Where's the mustard, please?
Up for a cruise across the seas?
Want to come over for a glass of wine?
Well, not today, but any ol' time
Yesterday would be just fine
Excuse me, is this stuff on sale?
Did I tell you my cousin saw a whale?
Are you going home right after work?
That car cut me off, what a jerk!

There's medicine I take every day
Hoping my condition will go away
My therapist gave me stuff to try
To gain more focus, and by and by
To one subject at a time I could stick
If it was a subject that I would pick
Such as sports or hobbies or a movie
Everything started to be groovy

Paul Jeffrey Davids

But then I started anew the videogame
Yes, the videogame is what's to blame
For the fact that I am not the same
And that I can't remember my own name
Because A.D.D. makes me less sane
Pass the pepper, it's going to rain

12. THE TV DIET

Listen, everyone, I'm on a diet
So don't you dare fry it
And don't even bake it
I just can't take it
Because I'm overweight
And I won't admit how much
But it's gone so high
My scale I won't touch
Because I don't want to see
What's been happening to me
By gorging on ham
Not to mention lamb
And all those trips
For potato chips

So the day of reckoning
Finally came
I don't want to die young
I want to stay in the game
And the only way
To keep the heart beating
Is to lose forty pounds
So life won't be fleeting

So like I said, I'm on a diet
She made me swear I would try it
Yeah, I'm talking about my wife
Who's a bit concerned for my life

She's set up a system
It's very high-tech
But it's turned me into
A nervous wreck

See, I won't eat a thing
Until I hear the bell ring
It rings twice a day
The rest of the time I pray
That I can starve until midnight
I am quite a sad sight
They say it's scientific
And you've got to stay with it
To monitor what you eat
Or you'll feel the pangs of defeat

But the best hope for me
Is watching TV
To distract my mind
Most of the time
From thinking of food
So to the TV I stay glued

I don't care what kind of show
They all amuse me so
Except for the news
That gives me the blues
Because most news is unbearable
And the announcers are terrible
And then it even gets worse
Because wars are a curse

Of armed conflicts worldwide
There's certainly no lack
And suicide bombers
And dopers on crack
And whores and seductions
Kidnappings, abductions
The news is gut-wrenchin'
So I escape to the kitchen
To the fruit bowl I prance
Where just be pure chance
A ripe banana I spy
I'm starving, I won't lie

THE TV DIET

One banana won't hurt
A diet like mine
Which is custom made
For any ol' time
And speaking of fruit
I'll have strawberries, too
And one squirt of whipped cream
And cookies? Well, just a few!

So I return to my chair
To watch which show?—I don't care
While at my snacks I slowly nibble
Hey, it's not much, please don't quibble!
And then an ad comes on
Playing my favorite song
It's a pizza ad, quite alluring
So now my brain starts conjuring
Lots of pepperoni dreams
And mozzarella schemes

So I talk to myself plain
Trying to ease the pain
That's pounding in my brain
While my stomach goes insane
A little pizza, why the heck not?
There's leftover pizza I like a lot
There's no need to save it
When I can microwave it
And stick it on a dish
With some chips, a great mix
And just one diet soda
And that's my coda

So to the TV I'm returning
And my heart is still yearning
To be skinny as a rail
So I can jump, run and sail
With my diet I can't fail
If I never look at the scale

Paul Jeffrey Davids

But this show that's on now
A story about a cow
And how healthy beef
Makes America the chief
Exporter of steak
So please give me a break!

Should I become a vegetarian
So I can live to be an octogenarian?
That means surviving to eighty
And for that, I can't be weighty

Hamburgers? Not for me
Steak? Well, let's see
Is it lean beef well ground?
Then perhaps without a sound
I could sneak to the kitchen
To fry up what I've been missin'
Medium well, no mistake
One terrific steak

These extra calories today
Will all go away
When I do better tomorrow
Hey, I can't live in sorrow
So while I eat my steak
I give the TV a break
Steak sauce, it's a must!
With lots of bread I can trust
One potato I'll bake
And then chocolate cake!

The next TV show that I see
Is completely food-free
But then what do I hear?
An ad for some beer!
Well, a beer would be nice
I could drink a beer twice

THE TV DIET

When the bell ring does come
The diet's temporarily done
Because it's time for a meal
Ah yes, let the bell peal

And so a big meal I chow down
Unfortunately no one's in town
To share this big turkey
That I serve with beef jerky
And carrots and yams
And peanut butter and jams
And for desert, lemon pie
What a big boy am I!

13. THE WEALTHIEST MAN IN THE WORLD

Cal Humphrey Corsican was so wealthy
That he had become rather stealthy
Because he had always sought
All that could be bought
And the danger was real
That from him thieves would steal
Because some things that he owned
Could not be cloned

His estates, there were many
They were worth quite a penny
The British castle on cliffs white
The Versailles mansion, such a sight
And homes by the dozens
For all of his cousins
And cabins in the mountains
And vast gardens with fountains
Paintings so rare
Tapestries fair
Antiques galore
And still there was more

The wardrobe Cal possessed
Was so extensive
His fleet of splendid cars
Astonishingly expensive
Private airplanes and jets
And yachts nobody gets
Unless their total net worth
Exceeds a fat Sultan's girth

THE WEALTHIEST MAN IN THE WORLD

And as for his private pleasure
He could spend all his days in leisure
In dozens of spas with hot tub
Eating a mountain of grub

And how anyone dared
To have such feasts prepared
And cooked to perfection
With every confection
For parties quite lavish
With ladies to ravish
Well it's anyone's guess
Whether he ever had less
Or how he had amassed
A fortune so vast

If one of his limousines
Got a small dent
Well, off to the junkyard
It would be sent

And if one of his rose bushes
Drooped in hot weather
Well, he'd have it yanked out
The roots to sever
He'd replace it in an hour
Lest the whole garden turn sour

And if one of his yachts
Was scratched by its anchor
Well, he'd have a yearning
Yes Ol' Cal would hanker
For a new yacht, much better
To sail an ocean even wetter

Of this man who had much
And still wanted more
You are probably asking
What was it for?

There were many people zealous
Who found themselves jealous
Of Cal Humphrey Corsican
Who had such a fortune
That every Arabian Prince
With envy would wince
When hearing his name
And contemplating his fame

They would take off a sandal
And fly off the handle
With such outrageous rage
That one cannot gauge
How a fair-minded jury
Would react to such fury

But all that Cal owned
And all he possessed
Was not sufficient
To fill him with zest
For powers he sought
That could not be bought
To rule his nation
Would be his station

To be the people's selection
He'd have to win an election
But he was occupied with his mistress
Having an erection

He had a philosophical problem
That some might think weird
As a ruler, was it better
To be loved or feared?

If he were to rule
And command a navy
Was it a benefit
To have so much gravy?

THE WEALTHIEST MAN IN THE WORLD

Should he conform to the norm
And pay his class dues?
Should he dress casually
And put on tennis shoes?

Should he become a nice guy
Or not even try?
And could he outlast
The hidden sins of his past?

And then he realized
None of that mattered
His opponents in the election
All would be battered
Because he'd buy the companies
That built the voting machines
The votes for him
Would fulfill all his dreams

Those machines he would rule
For Cal was no fool
They would vote to his pleasure
By every possible measure
He made them vote once
He made them vote twice
Three times, no four times
He just wasn't nice

Some say lust for power
Is the motive supreme
Some say it's sex
To exceed a wet dream

He bestowed gifts of fine porcelain
Yes, that was Cal Humphrey Corsican
Gifts for a lady he admired
A beauty who inspired
His pursuit of acquisition
In every possible rendition

Paul Jeffrey Davids

Whether for fortune or fame
Or power in his name
He could not abide
When the lady was not at his side
To be his main source of pride
And come along for his ride
But she was never to be his bride
No, never to be his bride

And what was her name?
Why, Lorraine Lucy Fontaine
Who arose from humble birth
Hoping to share his net worth
And her allowance that he bestowed
Was money that constantly flowed
Into accounts she controlled
If the truth be told
And yes, his power soon equaled
His assets virtually imperial
But there was a problem, you see
A disease venereal!

The woman he most loved
And the one he most ravished
The one he adored
And upon whom he lavished
Was not quite as pure
As he had thought her to be
Oh, why had he trusted her?
Why didn't he see?

For he had never once suspected
That she was lethally infected
With a germ so contagious
That its effects were outrageous
And in an insidious way
It crept in to stay
In the bloodstream unseen
Making his life careen

THE WEALTHIEST MAN IN THE WORLD

From Ups to downs
From smiles to frowns
And then his flesh erupted
He was mortally corrupted

He called every doctor
He took many potions
He swallowed medicine by the bottle
And even tried lotions

But there was no cure
For his terrible affliction
And as for his power and wealth
And every other addiction
It all came to naught
As he was laid low
By something so tiny
But something that did grow
From a germ unseen
Except under microscope
Into a malady ferocious
With which he could not cope

And as he lay fading
From this world of ours
He contemplated his estates
And his mansions and towers

He thought of his power
Of peace and war
And he asked himself one question
What was it for?

14. THE HOUSE ON THE HILL

The truth is
I often grouse
Because I am
A very old house

In history books I'm worth a page
I ache from use and advanced age
The families I've had number five
And one man among them is no longer alive

Near the shrubs that my roof does shade
By the trees where many children played
The path that leads to me is winding
And pavement near me they are grinding
To make way for a new sewer pipe
The house across the street? She's not my type

I was built in nineteen ten
Then in nineteen ninety, half-built again
Not to mention another expansion
But believe me, I am not a mansion
And if with my history I shall go on
The first family who lived in me relied upon
Every inch of my every room and part
To house their kids who did start
School at ages very young
They were smart and gifted
With talents unsung

Their family name was Upanishad
As families go, they were not at all bad
Sandra watched the kids, no surprise
Sanjai owned a hardware enterprise

THE HOUSE ON THE HILL

And that's how I got
My French front door
That for a century
Still does endure

Sanjai also built
My side deck
But my back yard?
It was a wreck

They prayed to Ganesh
And begged his pardon
They cleaned up my yard
And planted my garden

From India they hailed
They were both Hindu
They believed they'd reincarnate
And that all souls do

Reincarnation after a spell
Called a Great Sleep
After death comes calling
Taking souls to The Deep

To me religion matters
Not at all
Houses are like that
We rise, we fall
We are rather existential
We find that to be providential
Our stay here on this Earth is quite short
So the thing to do is: be a good sport

After a few years
I was up for sale
There was no smog then
You could inhale

Paul Jeffrey Davids

The air was fresh
The sky all blue
And if the truth be told
I was still quite new

The next family's name was Kuchinor
Ed Kuchinor installed my hardwood floor
And the leaded windows in my buffet
Were the Kuchinor family's way
Of impressing their attractive niece
They turned me into a conversation piece

The only pets
That they kept inside me
Were the goldfish in an aquarium
And a bird named Free

The goldfish in their tank
The bird in its cage
With calm pets like that
A house doesn't age

I was so very happy
Not to have frogs
And all the more glad
Not to have dogs
But cats, yes
They do agree with me
A cat's calm wisdom
Eternally
Radiates brilliant light
Soothing the night

There was no Kuchinor cat
But there was a rat
It lived in the dark
Beneath my floorboards so stark
It would often sneak around for food
Putting put me in an awful mood

THE HOUSE ON THE HILL

Tom Kuchinor was a passionate preacher
His wife Sue Anne, a devoted teacher
Tom was a master of every tool
He also practiced the golden rule

The decades passed while they lived in me
But eventually Tom was chosen to be
Leader of a church back in Maine
Being sold again was quite a pain
But with the years, my price inflated
My lack of pride then abated

My self confidence slowly increased
I was always owned, never leased
But it wasn't until three decades passed
When my future fate was truly cast
Because for the next family I did expand
To a second floor where you can stand
And see green hills quite far away
That family decided to stay and stay

Their name was Jones
A last name quite plain
But she was called Echelaria
And he was Zokomane

Zokomane designed my second level
And all my windows he did bevel
My banister was like a gift unfolding
Expertly carved for ease of holding

They had no kids
It was sometimes lonely
Echelaria Jones sighed and said "If only"
If only she had a daughter and son
Then life's great purpose would be won
But sadly she had neither one
But my expanded size was such fun

Paul Jeffrey Davids

My new bedrooms had been constructed
In hopes the Jones' dream wouldn't be obstructed
And a baby would come and then would grow
But it wasn't to be; it wasn't so

After awhile I was sold again
There came a huge family, numbering ten
The kids shared bedrooms upstairs and down
And all day long I'd hear the sound
Of footsteps clattering on my stairs
My wallpaper got lots of tears
And my shingles crumpled from young feet
Out on the rooftop in summer heat

Their last name was Hoppingdale
They'd bought me in a quick short sale
With all those kids and all those feet
My poor floors sagged and I felt beat

My fireplace always had lots of logs
And did I mention they had two dogs?
Watchdogs they were
Complete with scowls
When the postman came
He endured their growls
They scratched my floors
They chewed my doors
They gave me sores
They started wars

Those kids broke my windowpanes
I soaked inside during rains
So I was happy when moved they did
It was nice once again not to have a kid
Or adult either for nearly a year
I was lonely then, I felt fear
Because there was a time that I was robbed
I had nothing inside, I could have sobbed

They stole the leaded doors
From my buffet
I was so relieved
When they ran away

The fifth family had a mother-in-law
She was the sweetest old lady I ever saw
The children were grown
They sometimes would visit
The parents were psychics
That's sort of strange, isn't it?

The father's name was Eastman Doyle
The mother was Carlotta, who did toil
To keep me clean
From ceilings to floor
And she even oiled
My old French door

The mother-in-law?
Her name was Kate
She'd sleep in the hammock
And come in late
When dinner was already
On the table
She'd always light candles
Because she was able
To help Eastman and Carlotta
Prepare for a sitting
If the spirits were willing
This was all quite fitting

I remember a séance
In my dining room
I recall the rapping
Of a spoon

Paul Jeffrey Davids

Kate summoned a spirit
Who once lived inside me
The wind began stirring
Blowing my biggest tree
And leaves did swirl
And danced in the breeze
And a shadowy form
Appeared with ease

I recognized him at once
And I creaked in shock
It was Sanjai Upanishad
Carlotta took stock

I hadn't known
That Sanjai had died
Yes, if houses had eyes
I would have cried

Eastman asked
Why the clock did tick-tock
For that clock had been dormant
And its ticking did shock

The scene was spooky
It caused me some fear
How strange it was
To have Sanjai here
Because so many years
Sanjai had been gone
And yes, if I'd had eyes
They would have looked upon
Sanjai as a ghost
Who from the Great Sleep had come
To bring news of my history
From years long undone

THE HOUSE ON THE HILL

"Take care of this house,"
Sanjai said with great care
"Although throughout the years
It has seen much wear
Nevertheless, it stands proud
And yes, it stands tall
You are the fifth family
To ever install
Your hearts and your souls
Within these fine walls
And so it is fair
That now I do dare
To come from Beyond
To tell you I'm still fond
Of this house on the hill
Where we lived until
We could afford it no more
When we were quite poor
Yes, in those days we were poor"

How fine it was
To hear Sanjai speak
Such praiseworthy words
Which forever I'll keep
In my hearth ever glowing
When autumn winds are blowing
Knowing that I
A humble house beneath vast sky
Have a purpose for being
That will never die

15. THE GAMBLER

I won and won
All last week
I swear it was an incredible
Seven day streak
I racked up the gold
And now that you've been told
Perhaps you'd like to invest
Listen, I'm no pest
I'm at the top of my game
And I'm not to blame
For the sevens and elevens
Ouch – that's a damn shame!

Hey, Barney
You've got to trust me
The blackjack dealer's cheating
He wants to bust me

The dealer's a snake
But I'm on the make
I'll wipe off that grin
Above his squared-off chin

Because I am a gambler
Which means I'm always ahead
Okay – it actually means I dread
The true facts about what I just said

And the truth may not be rosy
But my fantasy world is cozy
In my mind I'm always on top
In my mind, lucky streaks never stop

THE GAMBLER

To the penthouse, I'm always headed
With a nice chick, I'll soon be bedded
A couple drinks we had before dinner
And in my head I'm now a big winner
But I never really do keep score
And I often tend to ignore
My losses that can be steep
The truth? I'm in pretty deep

Can you make me a loan?
Can't we discuss it on the phone?
I swear I'm on a winning streak
A short-term loan, that's all I seek

Hey, Barney, I've got the vibes
That's how I know
That what I put on the table
is gonna grow and grow

I've got a feeling, see?
Well, how can THIS be?
It's craps, and didn't I bet the line?
Snake-eyes will be just fine

You see, in my mind
I've already won
In my mind
Those dudes are done
And I'm already celebratin'
Cause I'm really concentratin'
But the truth is, well
I used to be hot
But now these five chips
They're all that I've got

Okay, I'll at last admit
That I am a stupid shit
And I'm having quite a fit
Yes, it makes me want to spit

Paul Jeffrey Davids

I'm gonna scream and shout
I've been wiped out
But it's no time to pout
Even though it's a rout

I just need one more try
It's do or die
I'll shoot for the sky
Why would I lie?

That's what I told the pit boss
I owe him twenty grand
"Would I lie to you?" I said
"This ain't no one night stand"

I said I play here all the time
I'm a regular player, sure
But the sad truth is
And the truth it be
For my gambling addiction
There is no cure

16. MISSING SHOES

When on your feet
You don't know what to wear
I'm sure in your closet
You'll find a pair
Of splendid shoes
That's the good news

Hopefully they won't be worn
Probably they are not torn
But you will mind
If they're not shined

So I certainly hope
That you didn't demolish
The shoebox where
You keep your shoe polish

But owning shoes
Is not the whole matter
For if by chance
Your shoes do scatter
Here and there
Behind the closet door
And under the bed
And across the floor
And in a drawer
And you find four
That have no match
There is a catch

Paul Jeffrey Davids

But do not sigh
You'll have to try
You'll have to look
Behind every book
And in every corner
And every nook

Under the cat's bed – Reach!
Even if the cat does screech
Or maybe you left them
At the county fair
Or maybe they're lost
Under a stair

I doubt you left them
In the garage
You may think you see them
But it could be a mirage

They could be lost
Beneath the house
They could now be apartments
For more than one mouse

Or perhaps they've trotted
Off to the attic
Or behind the radio
Where there's lots of static

Mischievous shoes
Sometimes hide in plain sight
You'll stare at them but not see them
A very sad plight

Or they jump into a cabinet
Behind a file
You'll have to look and search
For quite a long while

But don't get mad
Don't start to fume
They could be behind a broom
In any old room
My shoes once danced
Into the washing machine
And then into my sauna
Where there's lots of steam

And once they vanished
Into my dreams
And when I woke up
As strange as it seems
They no longer existed
Even though I persisted
To look for a whole day
Life can be that way

But without this turning into
A very long lecture
I'll tell you what I think
Here's what I conjecture
Go look by the roses
Because right under our noses
Is where lost shoes may go
When the wind does blow
Or there's lots of snow
Or the sun does bake
For goodness sake

And if they're not there
Don't tear out your hair
Check the hamper
Where they sometimes scamper
And then look in the kitchen
Beneath the sink
And in the laundry room
That your wife painted pink

And do not stop
To take a drink
Because this is more serious
Than you might think

You see, if shoes aren't found
The first time around
Then where they tend to go
No one can ever know
And then you will never see
Wherever they may be
Nor will you find
At any time
Those shoes so neat
You like to wear on your feet

But if there are four missing LEFT shoes
And you don't know what to say
Then before anyone comes and snatches
Those unmatched shoes away
And ruins your whole day
DO NOT let your determination sway
Without any interruptions
Follow these instructions!

Place the four RIGHT shoes on the floor
Neatly by the door
Then leave the room
From ten o'clock until noon

And don't you dare
Return too soon
Give things time
To realign

And when the clock strikes noon
Go into back the room
Where you put the RIGHT shoes
Hoping for clues

MISSING SHOES

And then look down to the floor
Things might not be the same anymore
That's what all this work was for
To have your shoes some more

Because suddenly you may see
Four pairs of shoes all together
Each left shoe with a right one
Such a great pleasure!

You may be astonished
You may be surprised
You may never have suspected
Or ever realized
That you should not get the blues
Over a case of missing shoes
Because they often find themselves
With a little help
From unseen elves!

17. THE WAR OF THE ANTS

Never before
Had there been a time of no war
Between the ants red and black
Who now ceased all attack

They all laid down their arms
And ants decided on every farm
"From now on, we can't
For the sake of the ant
Continue the battle
And all our anthills rattle
It is time for great peace
All destruction must cease!"

The cockroaches said "That's spurious!"
Oh, how they were all furious
They were shocked out of groove
And could not approve
The ant peace pact
Cockroaches planned their attack

Because cockroach commerce, you see
Had always been and would be
The instigator of ant peril
That would make the ants sterile
Because the more ants that exist
Well, that means ants will persist
In conquering land
Turning fertile soil to sand
Causing a cockroach rout
And driving all cockroaches out

THE WAR OF THE ANTS

Cockroaches like land
For in their massive band
They eat all they can see
And take everything for free

They want to everywhere probe
And take over the globe
And ants feel anguish
When cockroaches vanquish

But for a certain time
For ants all was sublime
The stems and the pebbles
That had been used by the rebels
To raid the anthills
To make thousands of kills
Were used no more
It was not like before

No one could say
What happened that day
When ant leaders held sway
In their special ant way
And declared that nothing tactical
Would again make it practical
To return to the conflict
That made so many ants sick
And that had decimated their ranks
To their leaders, ants gave thanks

Whether red ant or black
No ant would attack
From right mandible to left
From thorax to head
Ants meditated on peace
So none would be left dead

Their peace vibes had a long reach
And influenced mankind
For men and women discovered
That peace they could bind

And as peace vibrations did grow
For all men and women, head to toe
Going around the world
Like the waves of a radio
Black men and brown men
And yellow men and white
Took a cue from the ants
And decided not to fight

As it is with ants
So it be with men
It became a world of love
From the very moment when
Ants resolved everywhere
That for war they did not care
So all the world over, people too
Declared that war just would not do

No more bombing of towns
No more suicide attacks
No more destroyed cities
No more buildings with cracks
No more tanks and missiles
Only peaceful epistles

But indeed could it last?
It's best to rejoice not too fast
For someone always makes trouble
And the stakes always double
Have you noticed, a ceasefire
Sometimes becomes a funeral pyre?

THE WAR OF THE ANTS

Though the ant peace was worldwide
Cockroaches could not take it in stride
They plotted and schemed
And suddenly it seemed
That they would start a new ant war
You ask: whatever for?

The politics are simple
It behooves cockroaches to kill
And not just for the thrill
There is evil in them still
They want ants to terminate
And to self-decimate
They want ant peace to fail
And to turn into a hail
Of death and defeat
So all ants will be beat

Assassinations and bribery
Were the cockroach plan
Landslides and poisonings
And so ant refugees ran

Black ants fled into territories
Controlled by the red
And the reds made the black ants
This invasion dread

It didn't take much
For ant wars to recommence
Did this mean that the cockroaches
Would win a victory immense?

And as it is with the ant
So it is with mankind
If wars continue like that
Who will be left alive?

18. THE DO NOT CALL REGISTRY

How can I describe my sense of relief
That I no longer have to beef
About merchandisers who call
So many times it would appall
And make a reasonable man sigh
Because every time I used to try
To pick up the phone to call a friend
Some stupid advertiser would upend
My important conversation
To attempt his rude persuasion
For me to buy things
That I don't want to own
I used to have to shout
"Leave me alone!"

But thanks goodness for
The National Do Not Call Registry
Now there is
Such a perfect chemistry
Between me and my phone
When I am alone
I get a dial tone
And I don't have to moan
Because nobody ever interrupts
To get me to spend some bucks

There are, of course, a few exceptions
When I'm trying to make my phone connections
Once in awhile the phone suddenly rings
Louder than the church-bells of medieval kings

THE DO NOT CALL LIST

"Good evening, sir, I'm with opinion research
We wouldn't want to leave you in the lurch
Your opinion is certainly nothing to hide
And without your attitudes counted statewide
We would be lacking an important statistic"
Well, that kind of call makes me go ballistic

And what gives them the right to do that?
It annoys me so much, when I have just sat
Down for dinner, Thanksgiving no less
Along comes another call from an awful pest

And then, by golly
It happens again
I've just hung up on one jerk
And that is right when
The phone rings even louder
Yes, one more time
I'm getting good and ready
To tan somebody's hide

"Sorry to disturb your Thanksgiving dinner
But I've called to tell you that you are a winner
You've won a free sample of such and such"
Oh heavens, I've really had quite enough!

After four calls at dinner
And one for dessert
My suspicions are triggered
I'm on full alert

The phone rings again
But I'm no fool
I know what's in store
And my new number one rule
Is JUST LEAVE ME BE!
We're now having tea
And from that phone
I demand to be free!

Paul Jeffrey Davids

But it's Uncle Leo calling
From way back east
He's sorry he couldn't come
To our Thanksgiving feast

So the next call I'll answer
It could be Aunt Sally Sage
But wouldn't you know it
I'm suddenly filled with rage
Because it's another jerk
He sounds like a clerk

Well, I don't care for his obstruction
Or my Thanksgiving's destruction
This moron wants a contract
For home construction!

And the next jerk on the phone
Wants to clean my carpets
I'd like to drown him
In the LaBrea Tarpits!

Did I know my magazine subscription
Is about to expire?
Do I need a handyman?
There's someone I could hire!
Have I checked refinance rates
For my house?
How about an exterminator
If I have a mouse!

Political calls are not hot coals
Let them take our polls
And while we're on the subject
Do I oppose mink stoles?

THE DO NOT CALL LIST

And how about signing up
For a termite inspection?
And do I need some help
Getting an erection?

Excuse me, I say
I'm on the Do Not Call List
These unsolicited calls
Are making me pissed

But do they care
That they could receive a fine?
They don't give a damn
They act sublime

Sometimes I think Congress
Should pass a bill newfangled
Pardoning all consumers
Who have strangled
Telephone marketers – or better yet
Maybe what unsolicited callers should get
For their promotional elocution
Is simply something like – electrocution!

19. MY NEXT INCARNATION

If reincarnation is a fact
Then we ought to make a pact
To choose not just who we want to be
But WHEN we'll come back, do you see?

As for me, I won't be in a rush
I'll avoid the mobs and skip the crush
Of jumping right back to this ol' Earth
I'll wait awhile before my next birth

It's not that I don't like the spring
With flowers fresh, and the birds that sing
And it's not that I don't like fresh air
I love the mountains, I really care

But there are a few things
Between you and me
That could use improving
I'm sure you'll see

For instance: you're on the phone
And you have a question
Do you like hearing Siri talk
From some other dimension?

They should make
Some simple corrections
So robotic voices
Don't make suggestions

MY NEXT INCARNATION

If I push zero with all my might
I want an operator to hear my plight
I don't want a robotic voice to scold
And I certainly don't like to be told
That pressing zero is not an option
If I've got a baby to put up for adoption

I also have an aversion to war
Because I've figured out what war is for
War's about killing and mauling and maiming
War's about blowing up and containing
Your enemy who frankly doesn't like you
And his main goal is to kill you too

And lots of money
Is involved in war
Spending borrowed money
That's what war is for

And making profits quite obscene
While drones from the sky careen
Lots of corpses is what they create
While many towns they obliterate

And germ warfare I could do without
And torture? I don't care for twist and shout
And while abortion may be perfectly legal
It may not be optimal for your sequel

I also don't like big bombs nuclear
Or mushroom clouds no matter how spectacular
And radioactivity frying every creature
I'll skip the next show of this double feature

Or you could be a fertilized egg
But in the womb you can hardly beg
Your mother-to-be to please love you so
She'll decide not to abort your embryo

Paul Jeffrey Davids

And global warming
And pollution
And tidal waves
There's no solution

Hurricanes and twisters
And earthquakes too
Volcanoes now and then
What are we going to do?

Perhaps someday
There will be some futures
With no need for heart transplants
Who likes the sutures?

And there are a few diseases
On my list
Of things about life
That won't be missed

Cancer, M.S., AIDS
T.B., malaria and the clap
Blindness, deafness and heart attacks
And paralysis – that's a lifelong trap!

Alzheimer's, Parkinsons
And leprosy too
Schizophrenia, autism,
If your liver goes, you're through

And there are other things I don't favor
Debt and poverty? I'll take a waiver
Oil spills and insecticide
Starving kids that cried and died

And why are all these terrorists
Intent on blowing themselves to bits?
Don't they know that being torn apart
Really shits bricks?

MY NEXT INCARNATION

Rain forests clear cut to a parking lot
Carbon dioxide making it so hot
And is there a humanitarian distinction
For animals threatened with extinction?

So if it's like a lottery
Deciding when you'll be born
I'd rather wait than enter
A world I have to scorn

Forgive me if I want centuries to pass
Why not wait it out? Time passes fast
I'm hoping things will get much better
And typhoons and hurricanes won't get wetter
And World War III will long be over
And nature will bring new grass and clover

Bigotry and racism and plenty of hate
I hope won't exist for my new date
When I get handed a new life from fate
My future time to reincarnate
Maybe it'll be like a brand new song
Maybe folks will get along

20. MY TATTOOS

One day I didn't have anything to do
So I decided to get my first tattoo
I thanked the artist
Who wasn't the smartest
And then I paid
And went out to get laid
With Loraine who thought
That the tattoo I bought
Was rather inane
Because it misspelled her name

Well, at that I did a double-take
Because in fact there was no mistake
Lorraine with two "r's" was my mother
And Loraine, my best squeeze, was another

The two "r's" were quite correct for Mom
Right beneath my tattooed name, Tom
But Loraine (one "r") was in a daze
And worked herself into a rage

She said I should get another
That didn't refer to my mother.
And I thought, oh brother
More of me to cover

The first tattoo was on my left wrist
And Loraine, well, she was so pissed
So I went back to the tattoo place
And I said, okay, tattoo my face
With Loraine and a heart and a dove
To let everyone know we're in love

MY TATTOOS

I explained that this new Loraine
Had only one "r" in her name
So if you have half a brain
Don't make it the same
As my Lorraine with two "r's"
Unless you want to see stars

Well, the tattoo artist, he agreed
And with initiative took the lead
And after much practice
He added a cactus
And then put in the sun
And a roadrunner on the run

Well, this man would go far
He spelled Loraine with one "r"
And my forehead now is tattooed
So I don't have to be nude
For people to know
I love Loraine so

But one day last week
I started to freak
When Loraine went berserk
Because I'm just a file clerk

She met a rich guy named Freddy
And now they're going steady
I've been left in the lurch
Feeling like a jerk
With her name on my face
Not some other place

For a tattoo modification I was ready
Especially since I had just met Betty
Betty's was my next squeeze
She was the one to please
And for tattoos on my knees
I paid the full fees

Betty wanted me to cross out Loraine (one "r")
Which was probably much better by far
Than removing the tattoo
Which is painful to do
For when a tattoo is seared out
You may scream and shout

A revised tattoo on my forehead
Was swiftly enacted
But the procedure itself
Was rather protracted
Now I look like a document
That's been redacted

I'm all blacked out above my eyes
But on my neck a new name did arise
The tattoo says Betty in red and green
And Betty likes eagles, so her big dream
Was that I cover my back with an eagle bold
A tattoo that would stay until I got very old
And on my left thigh she wanted a golden retriever
And for my right thigh, we agreed on a beaver

Well, everything was fine
Until Betty lost her mind
Over at Lover's Ridge
She jumped off a bridge
And with her body quite mangled
And her hair all tangled
She was pulled from the river
It made me shiver

But Jeanette, well, she says good riddance
To Betty who worked for a pittance
In a flower shop
Where she'd always stop
To smile at every man
Who had a tattoo on his hand

MY TATTOOS

Jeanette favored tattoos on the arm
She said arm tattoos had great charm
And she thought mine were dull
She wanted a skull
And then she started schemin'
For the head of a demon
On my left bicep
So more tattoos, they crept
All over that arm
And then to my alarm
While in the tattoo parlor I slept
The artist he kept
Adding on more tattoos
Oh, why did I snooze?

Above me, the tattoo artist hovered
And soon both my arms were covered
With dragons and giants
And seven dwarfs quite defiant
And an alligator
The vulture came later

And as for my back
It didn't lack
Tattoos galore
I bought out the store

There was a joker for poker
And a lady cigar smoker
And clouds of smoke
Suggestive of dope
Floating out of a hookah
And a skeleton to spook ya
And a coiled up snake
That looked like a mistake
And the web of a spider
And a champion fighter

From the top of my head
To my ankles below
I was a walking and talking
Tattoo picture show
And the only problem
Was that I did grow
And the more that was so
What can I say but – oh no!

As the years went by
I was a poor sight to the eye
Because bigger was I
Why should I lie?

All my tattoos
Were no longer trim
As I got fatter
What a fix was I in!

The tattoos all stretched out
I was in such a stew
And my body hair
Well that grew too

And when I hit fifty
I developed some sores
My skin got infected
Around enlarged pores

And now all the art
That decorates my body
Looks like workmanship
That was quite shoddy

So as I reflect back
To the day I first got illustrated
I think to myself
Maybe I should have waited

21. INTERNET PORN

I think that I shall never see
A poem as beautiful as pornography
Which is free on the net
Whatever you want, you can get
No matter how gross
No matter how obscene
No matter how shocking
Or vile or mean

People from every nation
Participating in the creation
Of stuff you can fetch
That may make you wretch
Unless you are ready
For a diet quite steady
Of whipping and lashing
Of fisting and bashing
Or bondage and domination
And every abomination

The search engines are ready
To deliver it all
At one click of a mouse
Whether you're small or you're tall
Whether old or young
They expect you to come
And join their party
But it's not all that arty

Paul Jeffrey Davids

Think you must be eighteen?
Search engines aren't that mean
No, they never ask you
If you're just twelve or thirteen
All you have to do
Is learn a code word
Whether you're a dude
Or if you're a nerd
If you should search
For femdom or B&D
You'll see all kinds of things
That were not meant for thee

You can give a wink to a twink
But you'd better think
Because if the twink is underage
You'll be removed from the stage
Indeed, the law does warn
About child porn

And you might try S&M
As your search code
You'll hit the jackpot
You'll see the mother lode

You never knew people
Had so many vices
Until you see them using
Sexual devices

And as long as it doesn't
Cause you to frown
You can get off watching
Folks nearly drown

Yes, if death is your thing
And necrophilia is what you like
On the Internet you can find
Someone impaled on a spike

INTERNET PORN

Or if breath control is your fetish
And doesn't make you skittish
If you like weird mothering
You can find lots of smothering

And you don't need money
If you're searching on Google
Keep your spare change
You can be frugal

But if you have a bunch of dollars
You can pay for porn websites
That cater to your whims
And share undreamed delights
If grotesque is your passion
Whether you're gay or you're straight
Whether you're bi or a transvestite
You can still find a date

It's all there now forever
In the Cloud's infinite storage
And if you have nasty thoughts
It's quite easy to forage
Because we've now
Sunk to this:
Just one mouse click
To reach the pits

22. GRAFFITI

Here's why I appreciate graffiti
Because it tells me which gang will beat me
Whether it be the Avenues or the Crips
Here are some very useful tips

When they write on your wall
Don't try to stand tall
Yes, those walls with spray paint
Give a nasty taint
To the neighborhood
Where the boys aren't too good
But when they stalk at night
And give you a fright
Remember they think it's mandatory
To define their territory
With ugly paint scrawls
That cover the walls

And if you see them in action
Don't give a reaction
Just move right along
But don't whistle a song
Or they'll come after you
To turn you black and blue

If you paint over the wall once
They'll graffiti it again
Paint it over nine times
Then comes graffiti number ten

GRAFFITI

And this is the way it goes
The pace of vandalism never slows
From one generation to the next
They always can spray text
Of their gang's own name
It's a masculine game

And it may be a platitude
To say they don't like your attitude
It may be best to give them latitude
So you won't end up fried and stewed

You should remember to give thanks
When you watch them in the night
In spite of illiteracy worldwide
At least these thugs can read and write!

23. MY PAL, GEORGE PAL

When I was so young
I had hardly begun to walk
It may have even been
Before I could talk
On the television one day
A cute tuba named Tubby
Sort of whisked me away
Tubby was rather chubby

To his land of fantasy
In my imagination I did fly
There we were all together
Tubby, the orchestra and I

Tubby was shy
And was too nervous to play
He feared being in the orchestra
So in the story he ran away

He encountered a frog
Who became his best friend
The frog taught Tubby to sing
Friendship was a fine trend

And with courage and hope
To the orchestra he returned
And Tubby burst out his melody
And no one ever spurned
That brave little Tuba
Who finally found his voice
From that moment onward
Playing music was Tubby's choice

MY PAL, GEORGE PAL

It was not exactly a cartoon
A Puppetoon it was
Made by George Pal
Who made it because
Making Puppetoons was his profession
And here was his confession:
He made Puppetoons by the dozens
And kids watched as did their cousins
Because George Pal had a rare gift
Everyone's spirits he would lift
Particularly children, you see
Kids just like me

A Puppetoon was
Indeed a very special thing
Sometimes with music
The puppets would sing
They had no strings
They were not marionettes
But they danced to the music
Of tubas and clarinets

You see, this was all
A very special effect
And with awe and wonder
I did connect
With watching Puppetoons
From morning until night
George Pal was a master
At making them just right

There were ships of glass
And tulips that grew
There were orchestras
And marvels anew
Marching bands
And puppets in love
Flying machines
That hovered above

Paul Jeffrey Davids

And the great John Henry
With muscles so strong
He raced a locomotive
While folks broke into song

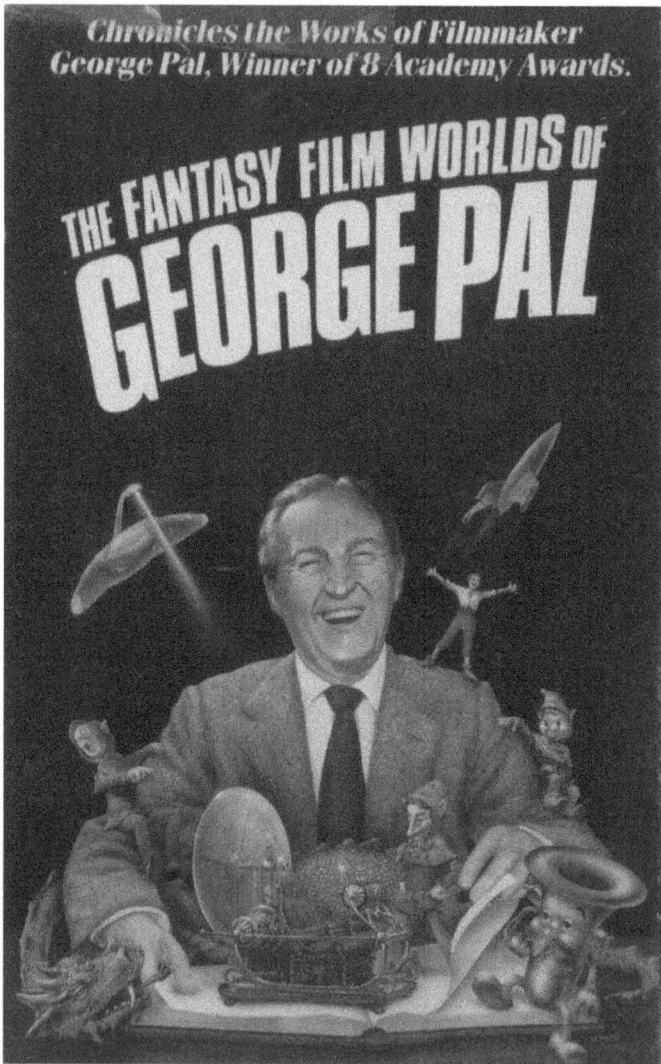

The cover of a documentary film about George Pal, available on DVD. Note Tubby the Tuba in the lower right.

MY PAL, GEORGE PAL

It was nineteen-oh-eight
When George arrived on Earth
He was like diamonds and rubies
I think that was his worth
His insight was mighty
His spirit was bold
And the stories he'd tell
All just had to be told

It was in the nation of Hungary
That George Pal was born
Imagination was his specialty
A man never forlorn
He kept his sights pure
His stories he would not spoil
With the textures of darkness
Until upon his native soil
Hitler's armies threatened
To envelope one and all
Then from far away America
George received a call
To leave his home and country
To begin his life anew
With his young wife, Zsoka
In Hollywood, it's all true

A studio called Paramount
It was one of the best
They wanted more Puppetoons
That George created with zest

So a team he assembled
To work around the clock
They made hundreds of puppets
And George had to take stock
Of every frame of film
The stop-motion was precise
Painstaking animation
The results were very nice

George Pal in his 30's, in the early days of producing Puppetoons.

George Pal at work on Puppetoons in Hollywood in 1944. Some of the stories were about an adventurous black boy named Jasper.

George Pal reviews a Puppetoon storyboard in 1944.

I want you to understand
This rare man, so please try
He had a marvelous smile
Always a twinkle in his eye

From George goodness flowed
He loved people, one and all
Attuned to a universe of dreams
He told stories of big and small
The biggest was a giant
From the land of the Brothers Grimm
The smallest was Tom Thumb
Who could dance upon your chin

Could it have been from angels
That George received his vision?
A bright light seemed to envelop him
And with never any derision
The Puppetoons were watched by everyone
Children especially found them fun

Never once did George Pal tire
And all the puppeteers he did hire
Worked ceaselessly, their hearts on fire
As George raised his sights higher

And so it was
Year after year
But then came a message
Whispered into George's ear
His mind reached upward, to the moon
Secret voices spoke to him, none too soon
For man's future destiny of space flight
Convinced him that to set things right
He'd have to create a rocket ship
He would convey a splendid trip

An early logo for George Pal Productions.

George Pal's first feature film, DESTINATION MOON (1949), for Paramount Pictures. The film quite accurately predicted what man's first trip to the moon would be like exactly two decades later.

Paul Jeffrey Davids

Into outer space mankind would go
And so his imagination was aglow
With a feature film story
Filled with glory
To the moon we'd zoom
In DESTINATION MOON

And so by nineteen forty-nine
George had begun
To make the film
That then did run
In theaters everywhere
Across the land
On lunar soil
Did his astronauts stand
Exactly twenty years
Before NASA's hand
Sent Neil Armstrong to walk
On lunar sand

It was the next level
Of the George Pal mission
He burst onto the world stage
Like nuclear fission

But his mind never slept
It continued to reach
And like the greatest professor
To ever teach
George Pal would not rest
He accepted the test
To show science-fiction
As if using the friction
Of flint and steel to fires spark
Imagination of future days quite dark
When Martians would come
And test mankind's mettle
In worldwide conflict
A destiny to settle

MY PAL, GEORGE PAL

Alien versus man
Who would make his last stand
With our flags unfurled
It was THE WAR OF THE WORLDS

A lobby card image for George Pal's 1953 masterpiece,
Academy Award-winning THE WAR OF THE WORLDS.

Ann Robinson, star of George Pal's
THE WAR OF THE WORLDS.

I was there (extreme right) as stars Ann Robinson and Gene Barry were interviewed by magician Brandon Scott for the 50th anniversary of George Pal's THE WAR OF THE WORLDS. The stars made hand imprints in cement at the Hollywood Vista Theater.

The dream of conquering new worlds
Did all film viewers seduce
WHEN WORLDS COLLIDE
He then set out to produce

A film in which a small band would flee
The Earth threatened by dark destiny
A planetary collision to destroy without trace
The past and future of our human race

And then George took up the theme again
THE CONQUEST OF SPACE told of when
A space station in orbit would exist
And of planets to visit there would be a list

MY PAL, GEORGE PAL

Beginning with Mars, the Roman god of war
Human destiny would have much in store
That would lead to exploration far beyond
This little Earth that is like a pond
In a great ocean of worlds so far we can't see
How it all extends into... infinity

What manner of man
Was this George Pal?
Who so many ideas
Did corral
As an offering
To all mankind
Insuring that
We would not be blind
And that we'd fathom
Our destiny
In short, that we would
Learn to see

*George Pal when he had several
successful feature films behind him.*

And how did his imagination
Lift him to such an exalted station?
To insure that the choices he made
And his determination never strayed?

There is so much more to tell
Of what George did
From the greatest challenges
He never hid
He created magic like a genie
How I loved his film HOUDINI
Then THE NAKED JUNGLE
With its ant invasion
The ants swarmed everywhere
A horrifying sensation

There was Russ Tamblyn
As TOM THUMB
And THE BROTHERS GRIMM
It was a plum
Bringing joy and laughter
To everyone
But the height of all
I will assert
Why not tell you
What will it hurt?
THE TIME MACHINE
Of H. G. Wells
The greatest story
That George Pal tells

He whirled us forward
In such a race
Showing mankind's future
At an amazing pace
Morlock or Eloi
Is what we had all become
In that future year
Eight-zero-two-seven-zero-one

George Pal seated in his time machine.

George Pal poses next to a Morlock from the year 802,701
on the set of his film THE TIME MACHINE.

OF **MORLOCKS** AND **MARTIANS**

THE **MONSTERS** OF **GEORGE PAL**

By Paul Davids

I first had the privilege of meeting George Pal in the fall of '69 when I had a fellowship for the opening year of the American Film Institute's Center for Advanced Film Studies, in Beverly Hills. I organized a retrospective of his feature films and arranged a George Pal Seminar, which Forrest J Ackerman attended (and which Forry wrote about in **Famous Monsters** 66). Several years later, my wife, Hollace Davids, coordinated a marathon retrospective of the George Pal Puppetoons as part of the Los Angeles International Film Exposition (FILMEX).

In the decade that followed, the last decade of his life, we were fortunate in being able to write for him. Every moment spent with George Pal was a time of inspiration, a time of dreaming and invention, of exploring the recesses of mind in search of illuminating and wonderful ideas.

We often wished we could have met George Pal during his golden years of the early 1950s when he was making one picture after another with scarcely a pause. In those days, he was busy bringing both beautiful and dark dreams to life for millions of moviegoers around the world, back when we were just trading in our tricycles for two-wheelers with training wheels.

LURKING IN THE DARK

George Pal (1908-1980), who left a wonderful legacy of fantasy and science fiction films, made a very special contribution to the world of cinema monsters.

In George Pal's visionary worlds, the beautiful and the horrifying exist side by side, dependent upon one another for their very existence. There's often a gentle and childlike aspect to much of his work, most apparent in his Puppetoons and the dancing toys in **tom thumb**. But undeniably there's also the demonic, frightening and terrifying—the MONSTERS.

Taken as a group, the monsters in George Pal's movies form a wonderful collection of bizarre personalities and species. A simple list would include

MONSTERLAND 39

The first page of an article I wrote about George Pal
in Forrest J Ackerman's Monsterland Magazine.

A sci-fi machine

Director George Pal
lauded for film based
on the H.G. Wells novel
that's coming to the Alex
big screen Saturday.

By Joyce Rudolph
News-Press

Science fiction writer Paul Davids will pay homage to director and friend George Pal when he hosts both the matinee and evening screenings Saturday of "The Time Machine" at the Alex Theatre.

Pal, who died in 1980, produced and directed the 1960 film, which is based on the novel by H.G. Wells. It received the Academy Award for special effects, and stars Rod Taylor, Yvette Mimieux, Alan Young and Sebastian Cabot.

Davids worked on several projects with Pal and after Pal's death. He produced the film "The Sci-Fi Boys" released by Universal in 2006.

The film showed how Pal and others influenced all the major sci-fi directors who have transformed the field into a billion-dollar industry, Davids said.

"The important thing for me is to emphasize how he was a beloved man in this industry," Davids said. "He was adored the way people adore George Lucas, and I want to keep that wonderful memory of him alive. He created so much."

Pal produced the film "Destination Moon" in 1950, nearly 20 years before man set foot on it. He also produced the 1953 version of "War of the Worlds," which also received an Oscar for special effects.

"Even today the film stands up as a great classic, so what I'm going to emphasize is how George Pal was and still is a giant and loved and appreciat-

Courtesy of The Alex Film Society

Actor Rod Taylor sits at the controls in the 1960 film "The Time Machine."

See MACHINE, Page A8

Los Angeles Times newspaper article when THE TIME MACHINE *had a revival at the Alex Theater in Glendale. I was asked to introduce the film with the current owner of the original prop of the time machine, Bob Burns of Burbank, CA.*

Bob Burns (right) and I describe George Pal's life and legacy to the audience who have come for the retrospective showing of THE TIME MACHINE.

117

I take a ride in the time machine in 1985 during the production of the Arnold Leibovit Production of THE FANTASY FILM WORLDS OF GEORGE PAL, a film to which I contributed.

MY PAL, GEORGE PAL

Well, there was a day
That came my way
Nineteen seventy was the year
At Greystone mansion, I was there
At the American Film Institute
Which was like my home
I was a student there
Long before I wrote this poem

I called George's office
His secretary responded
I was nervous indeed
I had never corresponded
With George Pal himself
Or with his office before
But of George's vast career
I knew all the lore
And I was persistent
With Gae Griffith, his assistant

She explained to George
That my great dream
Would be that my student film
Would be seen
By Mr. Pal, the master
Oh, how my heart beat faster

My film was called EXAMINATION
I offered Mr. Pal an explanation
Of how it was produced with AFI aid
And was the first sound film I had made

George Pal agreed to be my guest
He arrived at Greystone with zest
For my first film to see
And to sit alongside me

Paul Jeffrey Davids

He was then sixty-two
An age it is true
That many producers have ceased
To do what they do

But in George's twinkling eye
I could easily spy
A spirit and force
That never would die
For his pleasure he did show
And how I did know
That under heaven and Earth
That day was worth
More than any other
For my future to uncover

I'll jump along in the story
There were moments of glory
He asked me to write
THE HOBBIT, that's right

It was a film he hoped to make
Did Hollywood make a mistake?
George Pal was turned away
THE HOBBIT awaited another day

It waited in fact
About forty years
Requiring a new stance
When technology did advance

It awaited Peter Jackson's attack
To bring all the Tolkien tales back
First came THE LORD OF THE RINGS
And now in THE HOBBIT he brings
All of the Tolkien tales' things
Of Middle Earth
To a colossal birth

An unsigned letter George Pal sent with his submission of THE HOBBIT *treatment that I wrote with my wife, Hollace.*

The rejection letter from George's first submission of THE HOBBIT.

George made just one more film
It was called DOC SAVAGE
Unfortunately all the critics
That film did ravage

He tried many times
For one more masterpiece
But as for Hollywood
He'd had his last lease

He announced many times
That special effects were the way
To the future of cinema
That's what he did say

Effects, Not The Star, Make Many A Pic, Says George Pal

By WILL TUSHER

Veteran producer-director George Pal has come up with what he claims is a surefire scheme for imposing pay cuts on the film industry's newest breed of superstar — and there is nothing the Screen Actors Guild or agents can do about it. Pal's cost control program stems from his contention that special effects have been the dominant factor in recent years in many of the industry's top-grossing features — even in the big disaster epics that went to market with such flesh-and-blood superstars as Paul Newman and Steve McQueen ("The Towering Inferno") for boxoffice insurance.

There were potent, if lesser names, also in a pyrotechnic laundry list including such mighty turnstile spinners as "Jaws," "Exorcist," "Earthquake," "Poseidon Adventure," ad infinitum. But in every instance, Pal reasons, the special effects made the difference. It was the incident far more than the stars that turned on the public, in his opinion.

Credentials

His passion on the subject is matched, if not exceeded, only by his own considerable credentials as a master employer of special effects. Such Pal pictures as "Destination Moon," "Time Machine," "Tom Thumb" and "When Worlds Collide" have gathered special effects Oscars, giving Pal something of a credible pulpit when he sermonizes that it would have been possible for current special effects hits to achieve the same cataclysmic effect for much less money — millions in some instances.

Pal insists he is not spouting idle theory or indulging space age Monday morning quarterbacking. He makes a persuasive argument that he has built a career by demonstrating a facility for keeping the special effects budget down with a liberal application of expertise and resourcefulness.

He has, in various stages of development, a slate of 12 properties, in many of which he proposes to display anew his knack for achieving fiscal short cuts without shortchanging what ends up on the screen.

'Savage' Sequel

For instance, he has fixed a modest $1,800,000 budget for "Doc Savage, Arch Enemy Of Evil," a sequel in which he hopes to prove what went wrong with the dolorous predecessor he produced for Warner Bros., "Doc Savage, Man Of Bronze." This time out, he plans to direct as well as produce Doc Savage's comeback from a screenplay by Philip Jose Farmer. An independent George Pal Prods. project is envisioned for the film, which he says will be camera-ready before the year is out.

Similarly, his blueprints call for a mix of high-octane special effects and low-lead funding on a variety of other projects. He contemplates spending $1,800,000 in filming "The Last Revolution," from a screenplay by the late Rod Serling, based on the Lord Dunsany novel; another

Local AFTRA Bd.

Variety article of July 6, 1976, a year before STAR WARS, in which George Pal touted special effects as the wave of the future.

MY PAL, GEORGE PAL

The industry turned a deaf ear
Thinking special effects were done
Until nineteen seventy-seven
When STAR WARS would come

George Pal was the herald
His trumpet had sounded
Entertainment's future path
His message resounded

But nineteen seventy-six
Was four years from his end
There were several omens
Warnings that did portend

The doctors determined
That his heart was obstructed
That arterial flow
Had become corrupted

At that time a heart bypass
Was not a sure thing
Those operations could fail
And bring on death's sting

I do not know why
He went deep sea fishing
Off the coast of New Zealand
That news left me wishing
That he'd never gone there
And that he'd stayed home instead
Because the consequences
Were a sad fate to dread

Of beliefs there are many
And some not worth a penny
But this I feel in my heart
About how George did depart:

It was nineteen eighty
When George Pal's heart failed
And I feel quite certain
That straight to heaven he sailed

*I'm at the left, with Canadian Filmmaker Ian Paul Johnston (right),
at George Pal's grave at Holy Cross Cemetery in Marina del Rey, CA.*

24. PHILIP KLASS AND THE UFO

Philip Klass was a man who objected
To all of the reports that were collected
About unidentified flying objects, like discs
And he stated he was sure without risks
Of ever being wrong
In what he'd said all along
That there was not one shred
Of substance to the nonsense he'd read
Claiming beings from space
Were visiting the human race

So said Phil Klass
on many a TV show
That due to his vast intellect
He certainly did know
These were mistakes and illusions
And crackpot delusions
And it was all a big hoax
Yes, this was indeed what he'd coax
Listeners to accept
That he was correct
And that UFO's were a crock
Of pure poppycock

Time and again he made the crack
That evidence is what believers lacked
And he thought on his part
That it was courageous
For him to declare
That it was totally outrageous
To conclude that flying saucers were real
Or that they were any big deal

Paul Jeffrey Davids

That's what he did think
That there was no possible link
Between what witnesses claimed to see
And actuality

He would position himself to speak
As a writer for Aviation Week
His credentials looked rather substantial
But he may have had motives financial
To insist that all the UFO stuff
Was nothing but fanciful fluff
And that you were in fact quite dense
If you thought distances immense
Could be traveled across space
Indeed, for aliens, there was no case
And it was not at all right
To think that the speed of light
Could ever be transcended
All such ideas he upended

Without ever rising from his armchair
And without ever ruffling his hair
(Not that there was much hair up there)
He'd give you a chilling stare
And say he absolutely didn't care
What evidence you thought you had
Because all your evidence was bad
And he'd make statements outrageous
That were astonishingly fallacious
Explaining away every UFO sighting
As a case of ball lightning
Or a weather balloon
Misidentified by a buffoon
Or the planet Jupiter
Mistaken by people stupider
Than an average jackass
Or it could be just swamp gas

126

PHILIP KLASS AND THE UFO

He'd say "Don't be alarmed"
But he never charmed
Those who knew
That everything he'd do
Had one purpose clear
To scoff and to jeer
And to eradicate all fear
That danger was near
Or that horrific creatures
Shown in movie double features
Had any possible relation
To anything in creation

And he'd look straight in the face
Of anyone with a trace
Of belief in such stuff
And in a voice rather gruff
He'd say "It's all a crock
Of pure poppycock"

But his truths were quite elastic
As long as they opposed the fantastic
Claims that were made by many
Who never accepted a penny
To let people know
That what Mr. Klass said wasn't so
For it stuck in the craw
Of those who claimed that they saw
UFO's flying worldwide
UFO's that couldn't be denied

The witnesses? Pilots in their cockpits
Generals who were not nitwits
Scientists hardly in a stupor
And astronauts like Gordon Cooper
And Edgar Mitchell
Who walked on the moon
However, Philip Klass insisted
That none but a loon

Paul Jeffrey Davids

Would partake of such folly
Such utter nonsense, by golly
All those fantasies unusual
Contrived by the delusional

But things that Phil Klass denied
Required that he often lied
And obscured the facts
With his many wisecracks
As he'd do his best to erase
Evidence in front of your face
And he'd lose radar reports
Before contriving false retorts

There are some who believe
That he was on the take
That he was being paid
To say it was all a mistake
And that UFO's seen flying in formation
Always triggered official disinformation

And so TV shows one and all
To Philip Klass often put in a call
To ask his rendition
And to oppose the petition
Of those who believed
Klass said: "They are deceived!"

In this tale, a parallel I do see
An incident drawn from history
For when the unsinkable Titanic
Hit an iceberg gigantic
And it began to sink
To submerge into the drink
And people on the deck
Inquired if there was a wreck
And if danger was near
Some men said: "Never fear"

Yes, some men on the deck did the deed
Of seeking to deliberately mislead
All of the passengers confounded
Who could see that the ship foundered
Said those men: "It is only common sense
To label as nonsense
Those who say our ship could falter
Or that we're taking on sea water
And although for the truth you do thirst
Indeed nothing could be worse
Than believing this ship is cursed
There's nothing wrong here
And nothing to fear!
Now please, all the men must disburse
And to the lifeboats! Women and children first!"

The late Philip Klass, skeptic and debunker,
author of "UFO's: The Public Deceived."

Passengers who thought the Titanic was sinking
were told "Nonsense, you are being deceived."

*The alien in the 1994 Showtime film ROSWELL: THE UFO COVERUP,
about the purported crash of a flying saucer in New Mexico in 1947. I co-wrote
the story and was executive producer. In spite of government denials, astronauts
Edgar Mitchell and Gordon Cooper have stated: "This story is true."*

I'm with actors Martin Sheen (left) and Kyle MacLachlan in old age makeup (right) on the set filming ROSWELL: THE UFO COVERUP for Showtime. It was nominated for a Golden Globe for Best Television Motion Picture of 1994.

The poster for the French release of the Roswell film that I executive produced.

25. CLIMATE CHANGE

There are some who have the conception
That global climate change is a deception
And that rampant heat
And Arctic ice retreat
And typhoons and tornadoes
Like steak and potatoes
Are naturally served up
Like tea in a teacup
And that none of the incidents
Are anything more than coincidence

The Earth, some say
Has a peculiar way
Of going through cycles
It's no more than trifles
Because on this planet
When we span it
We find upheaval galore
And there's much more in store
That we can ignore
Because climate change is just lore
Simply a damned bore

Or it's exaggeration
Based on the false demonstration
Of polar bears sliding on ice
Or volcanoes smoking once or twice

And all of our frustrations
With temperature gyrations
And ozone holes
And melting poles
And lack of snow and rain
Yes, it's a bit of a pain

CLIMATE CHANGE

And as for animal extinction
We must make a distinction
Between normal and not
Because there is no plot
By man or God
To make sterile sod
Or turn forest to sand
And destroy the land
And make oceans rise
Or spoil the skies

This position you can take
If you should mistake
Facts and fiction
And declare with clear diction
That nothing's happening here
And there's nothing to fear
And the statistics we study
Are all rather muddy

As for me
I just can't agree
And I don't like being
Interrupted
When I assert that climate is
Corrupted

26. HAPPY BIRTHDAY

Congratulations, it's your birthday
You are a hundred and five
Tell me – what business do you have
Still being still alive?

Kings and queens
Of centuries past
When they reached fifty
Didn't last

Soldier and fighter
Painter and writer
Sought eternity's grace
But were all shown their place

The old grim reaper
Was never overdue
A century was the most
Anyone knew

But the ambitious many
And wise men few
Never had a hint
Quite what to do
To prolong life's
Extremely short reach
To instill meaning
That mankind could teach
To generations yet to come
When each generation comes undone

HAPPY BIRTHDAY

For death is proud
And death is fierce
It snatches us all
The short and the tall
The sighted and the blind
The cruel and the unkind

It plays favorites sometimes
For a few months or years
But doesn't it always
End in tears?

We pray the day
Be far away
We've work to do
Meals to savor
Places to go
Knowledge to favor
Planes to fly
Boats to sail
Mountains to climb
In wind and hail
Games to play
We won't be beat
We have victories to win
That are so sweet
We're busy right now
Come back a future time
Then our Maker we'll meet
Will it be quite sublime?

But ours is not to make the rules
We play the part of aimless fools
We horde some wealth
Protect our health
Trying not to worry
Always in a hurry

A birthday comes
A birthday goes
When will your time be up?
Nobody knows

So what lesson to learn
What conclusion to draw?
Life's frail foundation
Is our ultimate flaw.
And when to the light
We each do go
Many of us
Don't want to go slow

A nano-second
Is all it takes
For a blister to pop
For skin to flake
For a hair to fall
For death to call

Don't save your goodbyes
Until the hour is late
Don't withhold your love
By offering hate
Don't assume you'll be here
To right all your wrongs
Play your melody now
While you still have songs

27. THE END IS NEAR

The end is near
That's what some fear
A thought they hold dear
Because they say it's clear
That we're all damned
Except for the Lamb
And those who follow God's son
Whose work is never done

And those who say
The end is near
Don't shed a tear
Or attempt to peer
Beyond their belief
They feel their relief
And rarely feel grief
Because a rapture to come
Shines like the sun
In their gleaming eyes
Looking up to the skies

Perhaps they're right
And the end is in sight
Or perhaps they're mistaken
Well, I won't be makin'
Contradictory claims
Or playin' philosophical games
Because in my own way
I know what they say
Is correct in one way
That you'll discover this day

Because indeed it's true
That the end is quite near
You may soon agree
That I'm a prophet or a seer

For when you turn this page
Although you may rage
Because you want more
Well, there's no more in store

And you too will say
You know, he was right
The end was in sight
We now see the light
Because this is the last poem
In this collection
This poet is not in need
Of any correction
And so my friend
As you try to turn round the bend
You'll know without doubt
That this is THE END

About the Author

Growing up in Kensington and Bethesda, Maryland, I set my sights on working in film and television by age ten when I was an amateur filmmaker (of fantasy films with dinosaurs, dragons, sea serpents and other creatures) and an avid reader of Famous Monsters of Filmland magazine. I was a young teenage winner in the magazine's amateur filmmaking contest, sponsored by editor Forry Ackerman, who encouraged my ambition for a career in entertainment. After graduating from Princeton University with a major in psychology, I was one of fifteen students accepted to study on a graduate fellowship at the American Film Institute Center for Advanced Film Studies in its opening year at Greystone in Beverly Hills. Some of my fellow students were David Lynch, Terrence Malick, Caleb Deschanel, Jeremy Kagan, Matthew Robbins and Tom Rickman. While at AFI, I made a short film entitled EXAMINATION, based on a story I wrote at Princeton that won the university's Tiger Magazine Humorous Writing Award.

While on an AFI internship on a Warner Brothers film called DEALING, I met Hollace Goodman. We were strangers passing on a street in Cambridge, Massachusetts. The fact that we stopped for a moment to talk changed the course of our lives. We discovered we had gone to rival high schools and shared interests. About a year later, we were married and lived in an apartment on the beach in Marina del Rey, California.

I got my first break in film working for renowned agent Paul Kohner as his script reader. To help cover my salary, he arranged for me to work part time for director William Wyler, who needed help preparing to receive the AFI Life Achievement Award. Paul Kohner also got me into the WGA, writing for actor/director Cornel Wilde, and Carlo Ponti and Terrence Young. I also worked for my idol, producer/director George Pal.

I helped produce the original TRANSFORMERS animated television series. My credit as production coordinator for Marvel Productions appears on 79 episodes of TRANSFORMERS, and I wrote some of them, too, including TF classics such as COSMIC RUST, THIEF IN THE NIGHT, CHAOS and GRIMLOCK'S NEW BRAIN.

My film credits as writer, producer and/or director include:
SHE DANCES ALONE with Bud Cort and Max von Sydow
Showtime's ROSWELL: THE UFO COVERUP
TIMOTHY LEARY'S DEAD, a biography of LSD guru Leary

STARRY NIGHT, a fantasy about Vincent van Gogh
THE ARTIST & THE SHAMAN, my personal journey as an artist
THE SCI-FI BOYS – Peter Jackson surveys film effects history
JESUS IN INDIA, exploring the eighteen "missing years" of Jesus
BEFORE WE SAY GOODBYE, a Hispanic-American story
…and my latest: THE LIFE AFTER DEATH PROJECT, a feature documentary study of the evidence for life after death.

A few years after we were married, Hollace left her career in psychology and teaching children with learning disabilities, and she too entered the entertainment field. Over the years, she became one of Hollywood's most noted special event experts and has served as Vice-President of Columbia Pictures, Sony Pictures and TriStar Pictures, and for over fifteen years she has been Senior Vice-President of Special Projects for Universal Pictures. She handles all the premieres of Universal's major features.

THE FIRES OF PELE: MARK TWAIN'S LEGENDARY LOST JOURNAL was my first book, co-written with Hollace, with a Foreword by Stan Lee, an introduction by Forrest J Ackerman and artistic contributions from Sergio Aragones.

In the 1990's, Hollace and I co-wrote a series of STAR WARS books for Lucasfilm and Bantam/Random House, including THE GLOVE OF DARTH VADER, THE LOST CITY OF THE JEDI, ZORBA THE HUTT'S REVENGE, MISSION FROM MOUNT YODA, QUEEN OF THE EMPIRE and PROPHETS OF THE DARK SIDE. The books sold millions of copies worldwide in many languages.

In addition to writing novels and poetry and creating films, I am an artist. I create oil paintings, pen and ink drawings, and pastels. My art has been showcased in major galleries, and you can visit my online art gallery at www.pauldavids-artist.com or www.pauldavids.com

From PROFESSOR HACK HARDDRIVE'S™ POEMS, I created humorous songs, which are available on the Internet. Other of my comedy songs include YOU'RE THINNER, YOU'RE FATTER and WE LOVE YOU, WE HATE YOU, which are also included as poems in this book.

My more serious poems appear in RIGHT-BRAINED POEMS FOR LEFT-BRAINED PEOPLE. Another of my books of humorous poetry is entitled: POEMS TO READ WHILE DRIVING ON FREEWAYS (AND OTHER WAYS TO DIE LAUGHING).

Hollace Davids and I are residents of Los Angeles and Big Bear Lake, California, and we also spend much time in Santa Fe, New Mexico and Sedona, Arizona, where I love to paint the Southwest.

HIGHLIGHTS ALONG THE JOURNEY

My father, Dr. Jules Davids, when he received his diploma from Brooklyn College in 1942.

I looked rather young in 1972, though I had already graduated from Princeton University and I had married Hollace Goodman that year.

Hollace and I at one of the Hollywood parties. Hollace's profession for more than three decades: managing studio feature film premieres and the after-parties. The red carpet is always there on time, rain or shine.

The way we were: In the beginning, there was living by the beach in Marina del Rey and Venice, California (early 1970's).

*I'm the young cinema intellectual who had recently graduated from
the American Film Institute Center for Advanced Film Studies.*

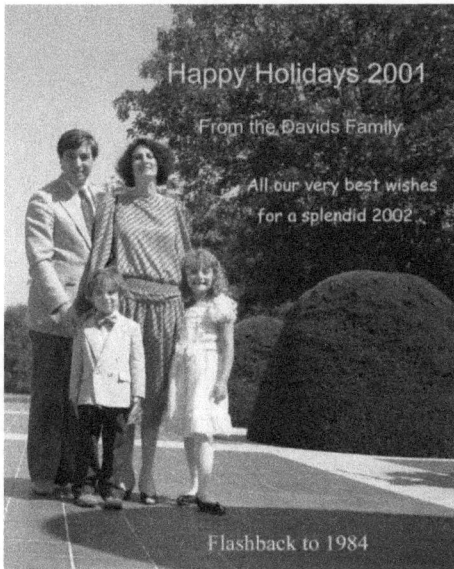

Happy Holidays 2001

From the Davids Family

All our very best wishes
for a splendid 2002

Flashback to 1984

*Our family in younger days from our annual greeting card.
Sent to friends and family in 2002, the photo was a flashback
to our visit to the Huntington Gardens in 1984. Hollace and I
are with our children, Scott and Jordan.*

A Family Western Photo in Jerome, Arizona in 1995. From left: my father Professor Jules Davids of Georgetown University(then retired), Scott M. Davids, Jordan Davids and me (as the sheriff).

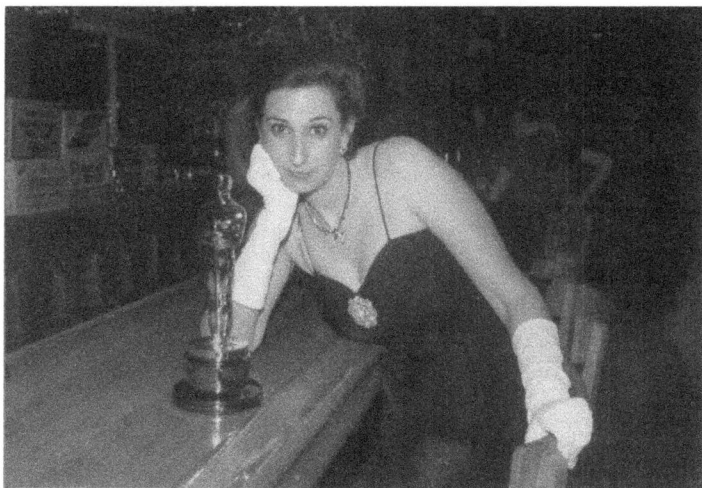

*Hollace with an Oscar. We always wanted one of those.
Maybe in our next incarnation?*

*Here we are looking very "Young Hollywood." Have we set a
record for attending the most premieres of all time?*

*I'm in Europe at the Slovakia Art Film Festival in 2004, where I was
invited to show two of my feature films: STARRY NIGHT and*
THE ARTIST AND THE SHAMAN.

*This was the first painting I made in college:
"Beatnik Leaning Against Lamp-Post."*

Part of a triptych (12 feet tall) of Times Square that I painted that was on display for years at Universal City Walk outside Cafe Tu Tu Tango.

Hollace and I upon winning the Saturn Award for Best DVD of 2006 for THE SCI-FI BOYS, released by Universal Home Entertainment.

The Davids family (left to right: Hollace Davids, Jordan Duvall, Scott M. Davids and me), the night in 2006 of Universal's premiere of THE SCI-FI BOYS *at the Egyptian Theater in Hollywood.*

When I was really a Sci-Fi Boy — that's me at age 13 (left) preparing a model skeleton for an amateur movie, with Jeff Tinsley (right) who made 8mm special effects films with me when we were kids.

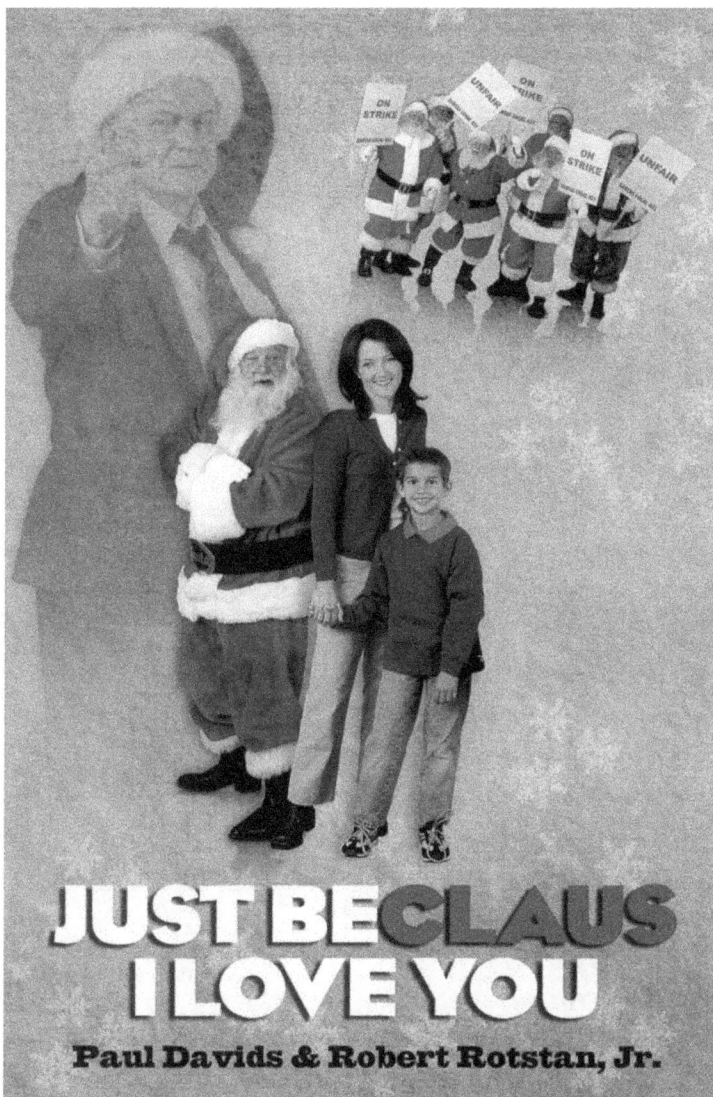

JUST BE CLAUS
I LOVE YOU

Paul Davids & Robert Rotstan, Jr.

A family Christmas book I co-wrote with Robert Rotstan, Jr., now available as an ebook online from Barnes and Noble for the Nook or as a trade paperback at Amazon.com Someone who claims to be the real Santa is living in Greenwich Village, N.Y., and he's writing letters to the editor about his existential crisis because the North Pole is melting.

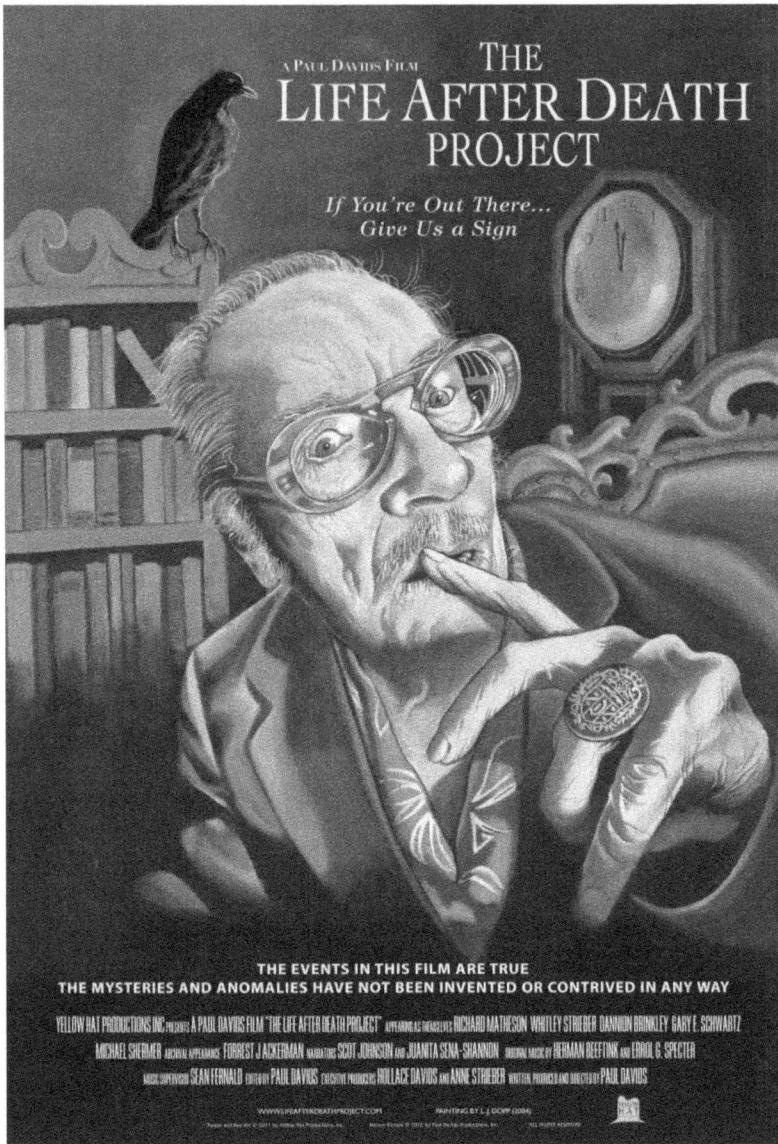

*The poster for the feature documentary (2013) which I produced and directed,
executive produced by Hollace Davids and Ann Strieber. The film
examines scientific evidence for life after death.*

POEMS TO READ WHILE DRIVING ON FREEWAYS
(AND OTHER WAYS TO DIE LAUGHING)

Paul Jeffrey Davids

Another of my books of humorous poetry. The cover is one of my oil paintings from 1999, inspired by the wild swings of the stock market, entitled "Bad Day at Bear Market."

RIGHT-BRAINED POEMS
FOR LEFT-BRAINED PEOPLE

Paul Jeffrey Davids

A book of my serious poetry. The cover is my self-portrait in Paris, an oil painting from 2011.

Printed in the United States of America

www.ingramcontent.com/pod-product-compliance
Lightning Source LLC
Chambersburg PA
CBHW021334090426
42742CB00008B/602